Free Government
e-Resources for Youth

Free Government e-Resources for Youth

Inform, Inspire, and Activate

Dorothy Ormes

An Imprint of ABC-CLIO, LLC

Santa Barbara, California • Denver, Colorado

Library of Congress Cataloging in Publication Control Number: 2016030070

ISBN: 978-1-4408-4131-6
EISBN: 978-1-4408-4132-3

20 19 18 17 16   1 2 3 4 5

This book is also available as an eBook.

Libraries Unlimited
An Imprint of ABC-CLIO, LLC

ABC-CLIO, LLC
130 Cremona Drive, P.O. Box 1911
Santa Barbara, California 93116-1911
www.abc-clio.com

This book is printed on acid-free paper ∞

Manufactured in the United States of America

Contents

Preface

As a professional storyteller, I have sense enough to know that the phrase "government documents" can make even a well-meaning audience of one glaze-eyed and fidgety. "Government" seems too complicated and depressing to contemplate and "documents" is such a very serious term for piles of paper that only an intrepid historian can love. Alas, this is the daily truth that many government information librarians face, yet a large number of them entered the profession in some strangely serendipitous way and are still at it 10, 20, 30, even 40 years later. I am one of them. I became a government documents librarian by default, am fairly new to the profession, haven't even reached year 10, and I'm hooked! Government information is messy, inscrutable, multifaceted, and, most of all, chaotic. Why do so many of us love it? And why would I want to bring this love to children?

I started working with government documents at the turn of the 21st century but did not become a bona fide government documents librarian until 2008. I had started as a part-time government documents technician at Southern Oregon University (SOU) with 32-year government documents veteran Deborah Hollens. I learned that the government documents department in a small university is a library within a library where it is possible to learn all aspects of librarianship. After I finished my MLS, I stayed at SOU as a temporary technical services librarian for three years creating metadata for our digitized collection of regional environmental government documents. Deborah encouraged me to apply for government documents positions and, in 2008 I found a position as Government Documents and Maps Librarian at New Mexico State University (NMSU) in Las Cruces, New Mexico. By that time I had a deeper appreciation of government information resources and had done some basic library instruction, a role that I really enjoyed. NMSU is a Land Grant University with a 70 percent depository collection dating back to 1907, much larger than the collection at SOU. I was called upon to teach specialized sessions in government information for undergraduates as well as upper division classes. I also taught a 3-credit information literacy class that included information about government documents. It was overwhelming to discover the depth and breadth of the collection and face the many decisions I made over the three years I was there. It also gave me an opportunity to delve into a truly historical collection and find the fascinating gems that made me want to share it all with children and young adults.

My first opportunity was for a celebration of the New Deal, "Soul of the People," funded by the National Endowment of the Arts and sponsored by the American Library Association in 2009. This was a nationwide outreach program to inform people about the New Deal Writers' Project collection, a rich compendium of historical and cultural resources. At my library, I was tasked with finding the documents in my collection that supported the project, creating displays and participating in the culminating community event, performing stories from the Writers' Project. Of course, as a storyteller, I couldn't resist the final challenge of bringing some of these oral histories back to life and I collaborated with several local amateur storytellers to do so. We interpreted several stories for the community event in an hour-long performance titled "Slaves, Sidekicks and Healers: Women's Stories Collected by the WPA" (Ormes, 2010, 17). The real gold was in the documents that I was able to find, both in my large hard copy collection and online at the Library of Congress American Memory website. The opportunity to delve deeply into American Memory and look for oral histories was thrilling and awe inspiring. It was really a lesson in finding the amazing materials that are preserved by our federal government. The ability to study these digitized documents from a turbulent period in our history when the government employed artists and writers to take down and commemorate our nation's cultural heritage was a privilege I'll never forget and I hope to inspire younger people to find the same appreciation.

The following year, in 2010, I had the pleasure of creating a centennial celebration for our government documents department. We had been a federal depository since 1907 and were overdue for the celebration. This time my inspiration came from a congressional hearing. Since NMSU has a very active military and National Guard program, I wanted to find a way to honor the young men and women and highlight the military, especially the contribution of Hispanics to the military. My opportunity came when, while doing a random search, I discovered a 2008 congressional hearing, *Immigration Needs of America's Fighting Men and Women*, which contained testimony from New Mexico native General Edward D. Baca, the first Hispanic to serve as Chief of the National Guard, appointed by President Clinton (United States, 2008, 23). When I first contacted General Baca for a speaking engagement, I had no idea that he would tell us a compelling story about Hispanic prisoners of war in the Pacific during World War II that would bring us all to tears. As part of the celebration I also hosted presentations by NMSU history professors and invited social studies classes from the local schools to come and explore our government documents collections. When I saw how fascinated the students were with some of the items in my collection, it seemed a shame not to find a way to continue to promote these rich resources to young people.

In 2011 I returned to Southern Oregon University as Government Information and Instruction Librarian. Since my return I have had the opportunity to work with undergraduates on their preliminary research projects and help them find government information sources. I've piloted an iPad program teaching with iPads in the government stacks area and introducing free government apps and mobile sites to students. In the process of researching these applications, I have discovered some wonderful resources that can work for both undergraduates and K–12 students. I am the librarian for several subject specialties in the arts and humanities and have extended my teaching about the richness of government information to those disciplines whenever possible.

Government information is an all-encompassing learning tool that addresses multiple disciplines and can spark the imagination at any age. This book is a culmination of my recent research and represents a way for me to highlight the many resources that I have found. My purpose is to introduce the reader to the incredible breadth and depth of government information and to show that it can be an exciting tool for educators at all levels of curriculum.

REFERENCES

Ormes, Dorothy. 2010. "Unearthing New Deal Gems: Telling Stories of the Great Depression." *DTTP, Documents to the People*, 38, no. 2: 16–19.

United States. 2008. *Immigration Needs of America's Fighting Men and Women: Hearing before the Subcomm. on Immigration, Citizenship, Refugees, Border Security, and International Law of the Comm. on the Judiciary, House of Representatives, 110th Congress, 2nd Session*, 23 (May 20, 2008). (Testimony of Lt. General (retired) Edward D. Baca, President and CEO, Baca Group.)

Acknowledgments

I would like to thank the Southern Oregon University Hannon Library for time granted for this project. I sincerely appreciated the support and encouragement extended to me by all of my library colleagues. Special thanks to Deborah Hollens, mentor extraordinaire, who started me on the path of government documents librarianship. Thank you to editor Barbara Ittner, who persuaded me to take this project on for Libraries Unlimited and ABC-CLIO. Thanks also to Emma Bailey, project editor, for her help on troubleshooting images and tracking down image permissions. Special thanks to Mary Alice Baish, former Superintendent of Documents, for her interest and assistance, and to GPO employees Kristina Bobe and Gary Somerset for providing GPO images. Thanks also to Valerie King, government documents librarian at Oregon State University, who read and edited initial chapters. Finally, thank you to my family and friends for their patience and understanding during the past year.

Introduction: Why Government Information? Why Now?

Think for a moment? Can you outline the intricacies of how a law is made in this country in a few short sentences? Imagine a game board with a snaking river of squares leading to a finalized law. Can you fill in the blanks? Google searching is not allowed. Would you go to Google to remember how to tie your shoe? Understanding the basics of government should be as automatic as the simple act of tying a shoe. Most of us have a vague idea, remembered from a high school civics class, but many of us would be hard-pressed to explain the complexity of federal government to an inquisitive fifth grader. Yet, in order for the U.S. government to continue to function with informed intelligence, it is the fifth graders, future citizen movers and shakers, who will need to know this information.

These same young people are becoming savvy Internet searchers, outstripping their adult counterparts in the understanding and use of new technology. But how savvy are they really? As they search the Internet are they able to interpret what they see; are they applying information literacy skills to fulfill the needs of their insatiable curiosity; are they able to evaluate the information they find; are their parents and teachers providing the guidance they need? Not necessarily. In fact, I have met university students who cannot identify and explain the Executive, Legislative, and Judiciary branches of the U.S. government. When it comes to understanding the functions of government, this is crucial information and only a starting point.

First there was the *No Child Left Behind Act* and all the changes that it engendered. Now there is the *Every Student Succeeds Act*, signed into law by President Obama in early December 2015 (House Education and the Workforce Committee, 2015). Whatever approach we take to education, what guarantees that our children are growing up as well rounded, engaged citizens with a lust for life and an abiding interest in science, history, economics, literature, the arts, and any number of other subjects? The relatively new Common Core State Standards that came out in 2010 are an attempt to address these issues. Adoption of the Common Core has caused some social studies teachers to bemoan the lack of opportunity to provide structured civics training for their students. Others point to the Common Core Standards as beneficial in demanding the kind of critical thinking that will make our young people better thinkers and increase their active involvement as citizens. As recently as March 2014, this was addressed in the popular press by an article in *The Atlantic*. Ross Wiener applauds the new standards for making our students aware of democracy through the close reading and analysis of three historical documents of the United States (Wiener, 2014). It should be acknowledged that these are only suggested materials and teachers are not limited to a specific set of resources. A rebuttal written by Nicole Mirra and posted on the *Washington Post* Answer Sheet blog by Valerie Strauss a week later questions the efficacy of the Common Core Standards in providing civics education. Mirra, a former teacher and currently a researcher at UCLA, emphasizes that the standards do little to encourage civics education beyond naming the texts to be used and provide no guidelines for teachers to create a dynamic literacy lesson on democratic principles and practices (Strauss, 2014). Lee and Swan also contend that although the new literacy standards applied to social studies can be a force for good, elements are missing that are outlined in the College, Career, and Civic Life (C3) Framework for Social Studies. They conclude that although the Common Core puts more emphasis on history than civic engagement it has created an opening for application of the C3 Framework principles and demands an in-depth approach to the discipline that was formerly lacking (Lee & Swan, 2013). Mirra and Morrel introduce another argument in an earlier academic article addressing the issue of civics education in the classroom. Their point is that the new standardization of education produces students, labeled college- and career-ready based on their chances of economic success in the corporate milieu, ignoring the need for students to be taught both the principles of democracy and the practice of it and the ability to think critically to function as responsible, engaged citizens (Mirra & Morrel, 2011). Despite this heated and healthy debate, children continue to go to school and grow up in this messy thing we call life in the United States.

The important thing to remember is that the Common Core State Standards attempt to create a framework in which to further children's education but teachers can achieve the set goals in a variety of creative ways. Government information resources can be powerful tools for teachers at all levels of the curriculum. When we think beyond the Common Core Civics and History standards and instead consider the integration of information literacy in the curriculum as a whole, it becomes apparent that government information has unique value. Government documents can enhance the interdisciplinary approach to information literacy that is promoted by the Common Core Standards because they apply to a variety of subject areas. This may be the educators' key to opening young minds to the variety and potential of government resources. Teachers bring their own individual expertise and intellect to the table and informed use of government information can reinforce their choices. Government agencies that provide educational materials are increasingly aligning their materials with the Common Core. Public and school librarians can act as guides to finding useful government resources and help bridge the gap of knowledge that exists at all levels of education.

Young people must learn about government resources at an early age. As they repeat the experience of using government information on a regular basis, they emerge from the chrysalis as fully informed, fully engaged, active citizens of a democracy dependent on the free flow of information and lively exchange of ideas. Just as a parent slowly and patiently turns over the responsibility of tying a shoe to the growing child, we, as librarians and educators, have the opportunity to lead children toward an understanding of government and to create responsible citizens in the process.

Fortunately, the Government Publishing Office (GPO) and the Federal Depository Library Program (FDLP) are there to support this effort. It is more important than ever that all librarians adopt skills for searching government information online. In the last five years, due to government budget cuts, a general move away from hard copy publishing, the demand for instant information, and new technologies to make it possible, the GPO has made more and more government information available electronically. The good news is that any citizen may access the information. The bad news is that only a proactive, fully information-literate citizen who has an innate understanding of government functionality can successfully access and interpret the information available. It is public and school librarians who, in taking full advantage of GPO and FDLP support, can make a huge difference in the education of the average citizen. As librarians, we have a rich opportunity to discover the broad reach of government resources and to expand our knowledge of the many disciplines served by these publications.

GOVERNMENT RESOURCES TO EDUCATE YOUNG PEOPLE

The purpose of this book is to provide simple government information search strategies and to highlight federal government resources that public and school librarians can use to help support the education of young citizens, K–12. Since much but not all of government information can be found online, the book emphasizes skills for finding and interpreting the online resources that are available. Each chapter is intended as a guide to a specific set of resources for curricular needs, including government search engines, government agency websites, and relevant apps and mobile sites. The book focuses on government information on education, the arts, humanities, and sciences and on the governmental process. While most books on government information are written for government information librarians, this book takes a narrow focus on the resources available to most public and school librarians specific to education, homeschooling, and the interests of younger citizens and their parents.

How This Book Works

Use this book as a reference point to jump-start your ideas. It can be read as a whole or you may find that only a part of it is important to you depending on the patrons that you serve. There are many ways to access and utilize government information to stimulate children's thinking. Each chapter of the book gives you specific ideas to put into practice. When you bring your own creativity into the process, the possibilities are boundless. Also, bear in mind that it is the nature of electronic information to change, so be on the lookout for new resources that have not made it into these pages.

This first chapter provides a short overview of the Government Publishing Office (GPO) and Federal Depository Library Program (FDLP). The FDLP has been the keeper and distributor of government information in the United States since the late 19th century. The chapter reviews the purpose of the FDLP and highlights some of the challenges and opportunities faced by federal depository librarians with the fairly recent move to an online publishing platform. It also discusses the Government Publishing Office (GPO), its former role as printer, and how it has morphed into publishing mostly online. Consider ways in which you are currently incorporating government information into your collection and how you might be able to enhance that use. Ask yourself the question, "What government information resources are my patrons using?" Only you know the answer to that and if you don't, it would be smart to find out if you can. The knowledge that you have of your patrons' needs gives you an opportunity to become a trustworthy guide to and interpreter of a confusing array of government agency websites and mobile applications.

Chapter 2 addresses the task of helping students and parents understand the federal governmental process. It focuses on Ben's Guide, a website originally provided by the GPO to help children understand the functions of government. You'll examine the new version of Ben's Guide that is targeted to both children and adult learners; and you'll learn about the various features of Ben's Guide, and how they can be enhanced by other resources to help older students and parents form a deeper understanding of the government.

In Chapter 3 you'll examine educational sites provided by government agencies, focusing on the accessibility of many resources using new technology. You'll find a section devoted to the information provided by museums using apps and mobile sites, which make it possible for children who are far from the physical museums in Washington, D.C., and elsewhere to benefit from what they have to offer.

Chapter 4 introduces you to sites that support Science Technology Engineering and Mathematics (STEM) education and the sciences; while Chapter 5 adds Art to STEM to bolster the concept of STEAM education through the use of government information resources. Chapter 5 also addresses resources in the Humanities.

Most of us are familiar with the U.S. Census, but many do not have full clarity about how it works. Chapter 6 introduces the concept that the federal government is interested in numbers at all levels and discusses not only the Census but also other governmental efforts at gathering statistics, all of which can contribute to a child or young adult's learning.

In Chapter 7 you'll explore the role the government takes in money and financial regulation. Highlighting the Treasury, the Mint, the Bureau of Engraving, and the Federal Reserve, it stresses resources that appeal to a young person's curiosity.

Chapter 8 offers you an overview of other useful websites and apps on the myriad different topics of government concern. You'll learn about the wide range of resources on the Federal Mobile Apps Directory and possible uses of smart technology as an educational tool. These resources range from an app for sufferers of PTSD and their families to Leafsnap, an app for tree identification. The chapter includes a list of favorite apps and mobile sites and incorporates suggestions for how to promote free government apps in your library through displays and programs.

Each chapter of the book spotlights a few specific resources that you may want to access on a regular basis, so you can feature selected federal government apps and mobile sites of interest on your library website or newsletter. Each chapter can be used independently as a guide to the particular interests of the librarian or user. The highlighted resources and featured apps pages provide you with immediate access to a single resource of interest. You'll also find suggestions for displays and programs that will stimulate your thinking about use of these free resources.

Know When to Contact an FDLP Librarian

Chapter 9 lets you know when to contact a government documents librarian in an FDLP library, when the question is more than you can handle. Although many online resources are readily available and many historical resources are also online, it is sometimes difficult to find and/or decipher what you have found. Knowing where the closest FDLP library is provides you with a willing ally in those times of need. Bear in mind that the effort to move content to online format began relatively recently with the passage of the *GPO Electronic Information Access Enhancement Act* (1993) and much historical content is either still in a digitization process or will never be online. Also, government information librarians are very aware of the volatility of the electronic information and make it their business to track down lost documents. They may have an answer to that obscure question due to this deeper knowledge.

Chapter 10 poses a question about whether or not it is possible or desirable for you to join the FDLP, outlining the expectations and parameters of membership and the responsibilities it would entail.

REFERENCES

House Education and the Workforce Committee. "Every Student Succeeds Act Signed into Law," accessed December 29, 2015, http://edworkforce .house.gov

Lee, John, and Kathy Swan. 2013. "Is the Common Core Good for Social Studies? Yes, But . . ." *Social Education*, 77, no. 2: 327–330.

Mirra, Nicole, and Ernest Morrell. 2011. "Teachers as Civic Agents: Toward a Critical Democratic Theory of Urban Teacher Development." *Journal of Teacher Education*, 62, no. 4: 408–420.

Strauss, Valerie, ed. "Why the Common Core Flunks on Civic Education." *Washington Post Answer Sheet*, March 12, 2014, accessed December 29, 2015, http://www.washingtonpost.com/blogs/answer-sheet/wp/2014/ 03/12/why-the-common-core-flunks-on-civic-education/

Wiener, Ross. "The Common Core's Unsung Benefit: It Teaches Kids to Be Good Citizens." *Atlantic*, March 5, 2014, accessed December 29, 2015, http://www.theatlantic.com/education/archive/2014/03/the-common-cores-unsung benefit-it-teaches-kids-to-be-good-citizens/284209/

SELECTED RECOMMENDED READING

National Governors' Association. Center for Best Practices, and Council of Chief State School Officers. "Common Core State Standards for English Language Arts & Literacy in History/Social Studies, Science, and Technical Subjects," accessed December 29, 2015, http://www.corestandards.org/

No Child Left Behind Act of 2001, Pub. L. No. 107–110, 115 Stat. 1425 (2002).

1

Stakeholders in U.S. Government Information

We all have something at stake when it comes to government information, as our democracy depends on a well-informed citizenry. Unfortunately, the average citizen is becoming more dependent on Google and other Internet search engines. Librarians are the middlemen who help to educate people how to successfully filter the plethora of information and glean the best of the best. When it comes to government information, there are two distinct organizations that help to make that job easier for us all: the Federal Depository Library Program (FDLP) and the Government Publishing Office (GPO). The FDLP helps to interpret the information that the GPO makes available. Both organizations monitor publications produced by government agencies in print and online and strive to validate, catalog, and archive important government documents. Most citizens use government information on a regular basis whether they know it or not. The trick is to help people recognize the value of this resource so that reliable access to it becomes second nature to them.

THE FEDERAL DEPOSITORY LIBRARY PROGRAM

Historically, government information distribution in the United States has been handled by the FDLP in collaboration with the GPO. The online *Catalog of U.S. Government Publications* (CGP) lists approximately 1,250 federal depository libraries in the United States dedicated to providing public access to federal government documents. Many house state documents collections as well. In the past, the GPO made these publications available to libraries in hard copy and shipped them free of charge to any library that agreed to participate in the program and follow specific guidelines. Just recently, in November of 2014, the GPO officially changed its name from Government Printing Office to Government Publishing Office, reflecting the effort to provide online rather than print resources for a large percentage of government materials. With the move to an online platform, the availability of government information has increased, especially through Internet searches. All library patrons will be finding the information serendipitously and will require help to interpret what they find. Public and school librarians are in a unique position to help with that interpretation especially for children and young adults. Some libraries may want to consider becoming part of the FDLP. Small public libraries and school libraries that may not meet the requirements can nevertheless provide basic reference help and act as bridges between patrons and government documents librarians who can provide more sophisticated support.

> A popular Government without popular information or the means of acquiring it, is but a Prologue to a Farce or Tragedy, or perhaps both. Knowledge will forever govern ignorance, and a people who mean to be their own Governors, must arm themselves with the power which knowledge gives.
> —James Madison in a letter to W.T. Barry,
> August 4, 1822 (GPO, 2011, x)

THE GOVERNMENT PUBLISHING OFFICE

The FDLP could not function as efficiently as it does without the existence of the GPO. Established over 150 years ago to fulfill the printing needs of the government and originally named the Government Printing Office, the GPO is a huge operation that once produced only printed government documents and now continues to print and/or catalog both hard copy and electronic publications. It is housed in four buildings just north of the Capitol building in Washington, D.C. When I went to visit the GPO in August of 2012, I was amazed at the size and scope of the operations that handled everything from straightforward printing and binding of congressional hearings to fine gold leaf and marbleized paper created by highly skilled artisans practicing ancient techniques.

E.J. Applewhite described the GPO in 1981: "This largest printing complex in the world has 35 acres of floor space paved in wood blocks. It processes ten freight car loads of paper every working day" (Applewhite,

Figure 1.1 Librarians from the National Library of Medicine (NLM) visit GPO and see a marbling demonstration by GPO's Peter James. Reprinted with permission of U.S. Government Publishing Office.

1981, 17). Of course, he was describing the GPO before the advent of the Internet. During my visit in 2012, I learned that the floor was created of wood blocks to sustain the incredible amount of weight of the machinery and to make it possible to repair easily by removing a single section of blocks at a time. Applewhite suggested in 1981 that the facility was already "obsolete and grossly inefficient" (1981, 18), and yet it has continued to crank out a record number of publications, even as printing has gone out of style, while public information access preference and budget cuts have forced a transition to electronic access.

Figure 1.2 Bronze plaque at GPO—THIS IS A PRINTING OFFICE.

WHAT GOVERNMENT INFORMATION ARE YOU ALREADY USING?

You are probably already aware of government information through your dealings with public patrons. Many public libraries choose to buy special publications from the government. Even if you don't have a copy of the *Affordable Care Act* in your library, chances are that you had at least one patron ask you if you did. Perhaps you've even bought a copy to have on hand or referred that patron to the nearby FDLP library for help. You probably have the *Affordable Care Act for Dummies* or any number of other non-government publications that grapple with the problems and promises of affordable health care. Perhaps, prompted by a list of American Library Association (ALA) notable government documents, you have chosen to download and catalog the free ebook provided by GPO, *Ponzimonium: How Scam Artists Are Ripping Off America*. At the very least, you may have the *Statistical Abstract of the United States* that, alas, is no longer published by the government but still is a most useful resource for government statistics. You will surely have Census information for your state. Certainly, you will have tax form information available and are helping patrons print both the state and federal forms that they need. The point is, government information is always cropping up one way or another and demanding attention from you and your patrons. Perhaps you are working with underserved populations. This can include adult nonreaders or people of color, new immigrants, the homeless, and others who may need your help with the interpretation of government forms, rules, and regulations. Whatever your patron base, government information will come in handy. It covers a wide variety of subject matter and stimulates both intellectual and intuitive thinking.

PINPOINTING GOVERNMENT AGENCIES

The fact that government information now pops up in Internet searches can be a great benefit to you and your library patrons. However, in order to feel somewhat comfortable with government information, it is important to understand some basics. The first thing to do is get away from Google searches and search **USA.gov** instead. There was a time when Google provided a government search that documents librarians remember fondly as Google Uncle Sam, but in June of 2011, Google decided not to support the search anymore. USA.gov, managed by the U.S. General Services Administration (GSA), has been the official web portal of the U.S. government since 2007. USA.gov accesses federal, state, and county government websites. Occasionally you might see an .org, .com, or .edu site. USA.gov is far more efficient than a basic Google search and does not necessitate adding a domain limiter to narrow the search to .gov, .mil, or .us. USA.gov also provides a Spanish version of the search at **GobiernoUSA.gov**, accessible at the bottom of the homepage.

The value of searching USA.gov is the focus on government agency web pages. The search helps you to determine which government agencies are interested in your topic. For example, in a basic search on *diabetes* and *heart disease*, you'll quickly discover that the National Institutes of Health (NIH) and the Centers for Disease Control (CDC) are agencies with information on this topic. Also you'll be able to ascertain that there is a National Diabetes Education Program within the NIH that has many online publications available. While in USA.gov, if you click on the tab labeled *Government Agencies and Elected Officials,* you will be able to choose the *A–Z Index of Government Agencies* to find more information about an agency. For instance, when you choose the link for the National Institutes of Health (NIH), you'll discover that the parent agency for NIH is the U.S. Department of Health and Human Services (HHS). Understanding the government agency hierarchy is a first step to efficiently finding government information.

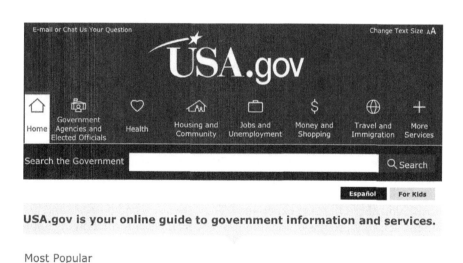

Figure 1.3   USA.gov search.

FEDERAL vs. STATE AGENCY

State agencies mirror federal agencies. If you find a federal agency that addresses certain information, look for a state agency that does the same. Adding the name of the state to a USA.gov search usually brings up specific state agencies of interest. Often state agencies are gleaning statistics from federal agencies or point to federal agency pages to alert the user to additional information. The important thing to remember when you are helping patrons is to listen carefully. Most library users don't know where to look for the information, and many may think that the information is linked to a federal search when in fact it necessitates a state search. A good example of this would be the current marijuana laws. While still outlawed by the federal government, marijuana is now acceptable in a handful of states under the jurisdiction of state law. When you get a question about marijuana law from a young person, you have an opportunity to differentiate between federal and state law and show both resources to advantage. (Of course, this book concentrates on federal resources.)

EXPLOSION OF ELECTRONIC RESOURCES: USE IT OR LOSE IT!

Understanding electronic government information resources and using them on a regular basis is the key to ensuring that they continue to be available. Now and in the past, government documents librarians have managed to keep up with monitoring the availability of resources through sheer dedication and hard work. As the information has migrated to online formats, it has become more difficult for all of us to keep track. Like any other business, the government tracks use and counts heads, so if you want to keep something, it is important to use it regularly, be familiar with it, and protest when it goes away. As GPO and government agencies make information available online, they are hungry for feedback on how they are doing and what they can do better. Almost every site features surveys to ask you about the user experience. They are quick and painless and just might help the process of making free government information available for many years to come. Consider adopting a site that you like and being the bee in their bonnet. Many citizens clamor these days about holding the government accountable for its actions. Government sites that have been developed for young people are a good place to start.

DISPLAYS AND PRESENTATIONS IN YOUR LIBRARY

Throughout this book, you will find ideas about displays and presentations that you can undertake using government information resources.

Some are linked to holidays, some to famous people or events and best of all; they are free and easily available. Get to know your closest FDLP librarian who can help you tap into useful resources. They can provide workshops targeted to librarians and are often eager to reach out and engage your patrons in other ways.

Work with an FDLP Librarian

Check the map of FDLP libraries and find out which FDLP library serves your congressional district (Figure 1.4). Get to know the librarian and take advantage of programs offered at the FDLP library, such as Census workshops or other presentations. Ask if the librarian is available to come and give a demonstration featuring specific physical or online resources. You'll likely find that the FDLP librarian is often able to provide handouts from the GPO highlighting government publications or websites. Also, you can refer your patrons to the FDLP librarian when more complicated questions arise.

If you work in a school, consider arranging a field trip for students to visit the FDLP library. Many university libraries are reaching out to K–12 populations, thinking ahead for recruitment, so it is in the library's interest to make time for an introductory tour, scavenger hunt, or in-depth presentation. If you have particular resources in mind, discuss it with the FDLP librarian ahead of time. A librarian who has no time for presentations may

Use the map below to locate a local Federal depository library or use the advanced search.

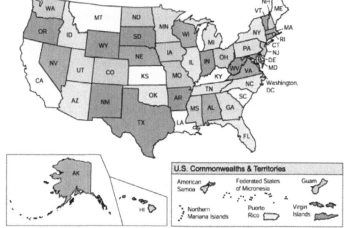

Figure 1.4 Map of FDLP libraries.

still be able to lend you materials from the collection for display and provide advice on government-related websites that may be of use to you.

FDLP librarians have a mandate to serve their congressional district. Most FDLP librarians make themselves available for these kinds of requests and are often eager to make the connection. Of course, they do have many other duties to perform, so it is important to contact them early and have a clear idea about what you want or need. Meet with your local FDLP librarian and share ideas about what you think your students might find interesting. Maintain an ongoing contact and build on the relationship over time so that you create consistency in the encounter. Since the librarian may see students only once or twice a year, it is important to find a useful way of working together and build on the experience by continuing the conversation and learning more about what resources are available.

How to Think about Displays and Presentations Related to Government

First, examine any prejudices you may have about government and then let them go. The young people that come to you have open minds are curious and have a chance to learn a different response to the possibilities of government information. Find a subject that you love and then do some research to see what the government provides. For instance, if you like computer gaming and are working with students who enjoy that, include some of the games provided through National Aerospace Administration (NASA) or the CDC and work with the students to play and critique the games. Maybe they can come up with better ideas and even submit them to the government entity responsible. This also gives you the opportunity to point out something that a government agency is doing and providing for free as part of a larger introduction to games and gaming. (Note: In my experience, most of the games are not terribly sophisticated, so this may work best for younger children or as an activity where they are paired with older peers.)

Nowadays it is not a question of whether you will be involved with the intricacies of government information, but rather whether you will be ready when those questions about government information resources come your way. The proliferation of online government information forces librarians who have been ignoring this resource or limping along at best into the role of government information professional. Starting with some of these basic resources for K–12 students is a valuable way of informing yourself while at the same time encouraging young people to take an active role in government so that they grow up to be an engaged voting public.

REFERENCES

Applewhite, Edgar J. 1981. *Washington Itself: An Informal Guide to the Capital of the United States.* New York: Knopf.
United States Government Printing Office. 2011. *Keeping America Informed: The U.S. Government Printing Office: 150 Years of Service to the Nation.* Washington, DC: U.S. GPO.

SELECTED RECOMMENDED READING

Government Printing Office. 1993. Electronic Information Access Enhancement Act of 1993, Pub. L. No. 103–40, 107 Stat. 112.

2

Understanding the Governmental Process

Information about how our democracy works is essential for stimulating the understanding of government beyond the political process. This chapter provides information on some easy ways for you to help students and adult patrons understand some basics about the workings of the federal government.

When it comes to skill in finding information, librarians know that it is important to use it or you'll lose it. We haven't always thought about that in terms of access. Much of government information is migrating to the Web and all citizens should become aware that the budget for this access is shrinking. Part of what drives the migration of government information to the Web interface boils down to dollars and cents. As long as people continue to access websites, databases, and apps that are provided, these resources will likely be considered worth the investment. If we are not vigilant, do not invest in learning about how our government works, or cannot answer our children's questions about government with some certainty, we're not using what has been provided and it may go away.

Some citizens are fully aware that congressional information is available and accessible. Others do not even think about it. Many college freshmen do not know how a law is made, mix up the concepts of Congress and the courts, and may even have no idea how to differentiate the Executive, Legislative, and Judicial branches of government. In a world where there are multiple distractions, children are pulled this way and that. When we impress upon them the importance of understanding the functions of government from a young age, they have a better chance of retaining the information and becoming sophisticated citizen users of government information. The GPO has made it possible to find lessons about the functions of government using the new technology that has become a powerful influence on children and young adults.

START SMALL WITH BEN'S GUIDE

Ben's Guide is a site that was originally developed for the pre-K–12 age groups, parents, and teachers (see Figure 2.1). Although it focuses on the information needs of children, parents, and teachers, it is also very useful for other adults. The old Ben's Guide for Kids site was recently upgraded and retitled Ben's Guide to reflect its suitability for adults as well as children. In collaboration with the GPO, the American Association of School Librarians (AASL) provides lesson plans throughout the guide to help teachers and parents utilize the information. Ben's Guide would benefit from a less text-based interface and more interactive functionality. Even so, it is a useful place for anyone to start the journey toward understanding the functions of government.

URL: http:bensguide.gpo.gov
Grade Level: K–12
Coverage:

- Historical primary source documents
- Branches of government
- Legislative history—how a law is made
- National vs. state government
- Election process
- Citizenship—rights and responsibilities

Figure 2.1 Ben's Guide.

Ben's Guide also includes Glossaries, Interactive Games, and links to U.S. government websites for kids.

Ben's Guide is one of the most important tools for government information that a public librarian can introduce to a parent. Often the parent who realizes a deficit in his own knowledge will start out as the primary user. The site covers basic information about the branches of government and functions of certain government entities, presented simply and divided by age level. Interactive and colorful, it is a positive entryway into the complex system of our democracy at work. Beginning with simple concepts and short text entries for ages 4–8, it advances through the grade levels to more in-depth information (ages up to 14+) and addresses the government in context as reflected by primary source documents.

Overview of Basic Resources

Ben's Guide is divided into three different grade-level spreads: ages 4–8, 9–14, and 14+. These are designated as Apprentice, Journeyperson, and Master level based on the ranks that would be required for the development of an apprentice printer. Thus, the site commemorates Ben Franklin's life in the printing trade as well as the original function of the GPO as a printing office.

Those accessing Ben's Guide can go directly to the *Learning Adventures* link at the top of the page or click on the badge indicating a specific age group. Parents and children can choose to learn about Ben Franklin and his role in the forming of the democracy by going to *About Ben and GPO*. Here they will learn about Ben Franklin the printer, statesman, and scientist. They also may discover that a printer advances through the levels of apprentice and journeyperson to master, just as they will be doing in Ben's Guide.

As the user moves from one section to the next, the information is basically the same, but is upgraded for the relevant age group. For the youngest age, there is limited text. However, there are not enough pictures. Perhaps in future the GPO will add some images to illustrate the different branches of government. Some extra links leading out of Ben's Guide help with this need. The previous version of Ben's Guide featured interactive games available on all four levels. As of this writing, there seems to be only two interactive games for all levels, *Branch-O-Mania*, which has to do with learning about the branches of government, and *Place the States,* a challenge for children to move the shapes of the states into their proper places on a map of the United States. *Place the States* is a game that was part of the old Ben's Guide and was added to the new site in January of 2016. There are also some printable activities such as crossword puzzles and word searches that have recently been added. The GPO intends to continue to enhance the site and eventually there will probably be more interactivity available. Throughout the site, you'll find parent/teacher guides to lesson plans and other resources.

For ages 4–8, links are provided to the text of historical primary resource documents such as the Declaration of Independence, the Articles of Confederation, the Constitution, and the Bill of Rights. Note also the concise text about how laws are made, a basic introduction to the functions of government. At this level, students glimpse the concepts of citizenship and the election process. They also learn to differentiate between the roles of national and state governments.

Ages 9–13 have access to the same information as ages 4–8. However, as they explore the branches of government, they receive added information about checks and balances in government and a basic history of the development of the three branches of government. At any point they can test themselves by playing the interactive game *Branch-O-Mania*. Students at this level also learn to trace a law from its introduction as a bill in Congress to the final signature or veto. Glossaries help them understand the terminology used to describe facets of law. For ages 14+, much of the previous level is reviewed. *The Federalist Papers* are added as a primary source to encourage students to begin thinking about the interpretation of the Constitution and the intentions of the Founding Fathers.

Moving up the Learning Ladder

A good example of the progression possible for a growing student is the section on *How Laws Are Made*, found at the 4–8, 9–13, and 14+ levels. Students 4–8 years of age, after learning about the branches of government and identifying the Legislative branch, begin to learn the concepts of legislation in the section *How Laws Are Made*. This section is followed by *The Election Process: The What and Who of Elections*, helping the student understand how the states are represented in the Senate and the House. There is a very simple explanation of voting and the election process.

The middle school age group (9–13) can start by getting an understanding of the difference between state and federal law in the newly added section, *Federal vs. State Government*. After reviewing the *Branches of Government* section, they can read *How Laws Are Made: Language of the Law* to discover a glossary of terminology related to the law and begin to get a sense of the path of a bill through Congress. This same page in the old Ben's Guide provided a step-by-step blueprint to the bill history of the International Dolphin Conservation Act. In the new Ben's Guide, this feature has been eliminated in favor of a straightforward explanation of terms. The strength of the earlier version was that students could get more emotionally involved with the material and the images at the site. (Unfortunately, the new Ben's Guide as it has first rolled out suffers from an overly linear, text-heavy approach.) The links given at the bottom of the 9–13 *How Laws Are Made* section lead to glossaries of terms from the Senate and Congress.gov as well as House Document 108–94, "Our American Government." This may be useful for the extremely curious and intrepid child or a parent looking for more sophisticated information. But what is currently missing is the "heart" of government that was provided in the previous edition by the focus on the Dolphin Conservation Act. A teacher, parent, or librarian can bring back that "heart" by doing a bit of research using some of the advanced sources that are discussed later in this chapter to find some important government legislation unique to the individual child. This can be very beneficial in that it allows the teacher or parent to tailor the information to the child.

By the 14+ age level in the section *How Laws Are Made: Tracking a Bill from Beginning to End*, the student can learn how the bill is introduced and sent to committee for study and public hearing. The bill eventually is voted on by the House and is announced in the Senate. Again the bill goes to committee and is studied and opened to public hearings. Eventually there is a vote and the bill is moved into conference committee, where any differences between the opinions of the two houses are worked out. Finally, it is enrolled (printed by the Government Publishing Office) and sent on to the President for signature or veto.

The International Dolphin Conservation Program Act became Public Law 105–42. At level 14+, a parent or more sophisticated student can read *Tracking a Bill from Beginning to End* and find the link to the Federal Digital System (FDsys) page to find out more about this process. In the earlier version of Ben's Guide, users could actually look at the final version of the public law related to the International Dolphin Conservation Program Act by linking directly to the FDsys database and looking for the 105th Congress, Public Law 105–42. Perhaps this feature will be added to the site later on. However, users can still perform this search on their own by following the FDsys link and then choosing *Public and Private Laws* from the list at the right side of the FDsys page. On the next page, choose 105th Congress, Public Law and then the + next to 0–99. Find number 105–42. The law is accessible as a PDF file and it is possible to download and print the 19-page document. After you have downloaded the document, look for the signature at the top of the PDF file that guarantees authenticity. This same signature appears on many electronic government documents downloaded from the FDsys database (see Figure 2.2).

AUTHENTICATED
U.S. GOVERNMENT
INFORMATION

GPO

The Seal of Authenticity enables the
viewer to verify the authentic nature
of a particular document, ensuring that
the content has remained unchanged
since GPO first authenticated it.

Figure 2.2   Authentication in
FDsys.

Currently students are given access through Ben's Guide to Senate Document 105–14; *How Our Laws Are Made*, a dense, 55-page detailed explanation of the process. In future the GPO should rethink this current version of Ben's Guide and include more information that appeals to students' insatiable curiosity and gives an experience of an actual law, not mere explanation.

Parent/Teacher Guidance

Finally, don't miss the guide for parents and teachers on how to use Ben's Guide as a tool for learning. Look for it as an icon at the top right of the screen, next to the search box. Here, parents and teachers can find links to online curriculum from government agencies such as the Smithsonian Institution, Census Department, Education Department, Educational Resources Information Center, National Archives, and many more. There are also information and lesson plans provided by the AASL. Many games can be found at the *Kids.gov* link. For instance, for children who are fascinated by coins, there are interactive games focused on the U.S. Mint at the link called *H.I.P. Pocket Change* (history in your pocket). It takes some drilling down into the *Kids.gov* site to find this, but look in the list of categories for *Money* and *Fun Games about Money*. *H.I.P. Pocket Change* gives children the opportunity to learn the history of the U.S. Mint and also to study history through a favorite interest, the coin. Study the *Kids.gov* site carefully and you'll likely find more useful resources. It is a treasure trove of information and enjoyment for children.

Practical Use of Ben's Guide

A librarian, teacher, or parent introducing a child to Ben's Guide generally knows best what the child may respond to in terms of text, images, and interactivity. It is important to know your resource and know your child or at least understand the age group. The GPO has tested the site on one group of 9- to 11-year-olds and a second group of 12- to 14-year-olds, but the real test is yet to come.

First, go through the resources yourself, read the text, follow the links, play the games, and discover the glitches. Be aware that, no matter what it looks like today, it is likely to change for better or worse in the future; but it can be improved with your thoughtful feedback. The site will continue to develop, especially if the GPO receives feedback from users. Be sure to use the *Feedback* link at the top of the main page to send your thoughts for improvement to the GPO. The important thing is to focus on what you want your children to learn.

For adults who are new to the United States, the map icon at the top right of the home screen links to citizenship resources, including the *Citizenship toolkit*. Once a patron has linked out from the Ben's Guide site to the U.S. Citizenship and Immigration Services, there are resources available in several languages, accessible by linking through the "Other Languages" tab. Public librarians will want to explore these options before showing a patron these services. If the patron speaks English well, Ben's Guide may be useful in many ways to teach basic information about the U.S. government.

BECOME A SOPHISTICATE WITH FDSYS

Sponsored by the U.S. Government Publishing Office (GPO), **FDsys**, the Federal Digital System, is the official search engine for authenticated online government information. It contains information from all branches of government.

> **URL:** http://www.gpo.gov/fdsys/
> **Grade Level:** 9–12 with guidance/adult
> **Selected Coverage:**
>
> - FDsys Advanced search of congressional publications
> - Constitution of the United States of America analysis and interpretation
> - President John F. Kennedy assassination records collection
> - Records of the Watergate Special Prosecution
> - Browse congressional committees
> - Compilation of presidential documents 1993–current
> - Public and private laws

FDsys is a search engine provided by the GPO intended to cover publications from the three branches of the federal government: Executive, Legislative, and Judicial. It also acts as a preservation repository of these materials, and the documents are authenticated with a digital signature (see Figure 2.2). Patrons can read more about FDsys by linking to *About FDsys* on the FDsys home page. FDsys has been created for the sophisticated searcher. Above are listed some of the resources specific to understanding the governmental process as well as specialized documents that are of interest to educators such as the records of the *Watergate Special Prosecution*.

When making a choice to search on FDsys, users would be wise to enter the *Advanced Search* area and limit results to specific documents or agencies. A basic search can be entered in the Google-type box on the homepage, but there is a link to the *Advanced Search* right next to the box. If the user enters a search on the basic search, it is possible to limit after the search results show by going to the limiters on the left-hand side of the screen. Users can also limit within the results. Since FDsys is searching full text of PDF files, it is possible to open the file and search within the PDF as well. This kind of sophisticated searching is beyond the skills of lower grades. Student access should be guided by a parent or librarian already familiar with the search method. However, the site is very flexible and will especially appeal to high school students.

Sample Search in FDsys

When I teach FDsys to freshmen at the university, I encourage them to limit to the use of congressional hearings. As previously illustrated with Ben's Guide, government hearings are a good starting place for students to learn about the workings of government. They are primary source documents and often they address controversial topics, documenting different points of view. They are also full-text searchable in FDsys. If a student is researching global warming and its effect on our oceans, I suggest an advanced FDsys search using the terms "global warming" and "ocean." A link to the FDsys *Advanced Search* can be found to the right of the search box. Within the *Advanced Search* it is possible to choose a collection. In this case I would have the student choose only *Congressional Hearings*. After highlighting the collection, the student then clicks on "add" and the collection appears under the *Selected Collections*. In the iPad example the collection is marked with a blue check (see Figure 2.3). Then the student can enter the search terms in the box directly below ("global warming" ocean). Once the search is executed the student will see a list of hearings ranked by relevance. If the student is interested in searching for another term, he can search within the results by checking the *Within Results* box and adding the new term in the search box. The user may also choose to limit results by year choosing from the *Date Published* parameters at the left of the screen. All other limiting possibilities can be found in this location. I generally do not encourage my students to limit too soon. I want them to see the various results and understand the breadth and depth of the topic. For this particular search, a student immediately sees that there are 1,000 hearings having something to do with the keyword terms and the most relevant one dates to 2008. This gives the student some perspective on just how long the government has recognized and tried to address the problem of global warming. In this case, if we search *Within Results* for "Oregon," we'll see that there are still 811 hearings listed and the same hearing rises to the top of the relevancy ranking, "Rising Tides, Rising Temperatures: Global Warming's Impacts on the Oceans."

It is now time to take a look at the hearing "Rising Tides, Rising Temperatures: Global Warming's Impacts on the Oceans." To access the PDF, the student can click on the title. Ask your students to look carefully at the title page, notice the committee involved, whether

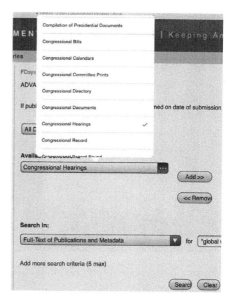

Figure 2.3 FDsys Congressional Hearing search on iPad.

it is a House or Senate hearing and the date. Then have them look at the Table of Contents. This is where you find the stakeholders, a list of congressmen and witnesses giving evidence about the problem. You might point out that Jane Lubchenco, a zoologist from Oregon State University, is giving evidence. Here is an example of an expert in the field sharing knowledge about an issue. Suggest to the students that they may want to look at more of this woman's work. However, some of the most useful materials for the students come at the end of the Table of Contents in the form of addendum materials such as white papers, government reports, news articles, charts, tables, and graphs. In this particular hearing there is a white paper by Jane Lubchenco. In many hearings there are multiple addendums of interest. Once they are viewing the PDF of the document, students have the option to search for another term within the PDF using the "Find" option on the computer. Not surprisingly, the phrase "climate change" appears over 50 times in this document.

Students will be tempted to limit to the most recent publications or may decide to change the relevance search to a "newest to oldest" ranking. For this reason, they need careful guidance to help them understand the importance of not cutting results out too early so as to be able to realize the historical aspects of an issue and the differences between relevancy and currency. Discerning students will find this search fascinating. If they want

Figure 2.4 FDsys Congressional Record search on iPad.

to add another collection, you can suggest adding *GAO Report and Comptroller General Decisions*. The Government Accountability Office (GAO) reports are useful for students because they are specifically targeted to a particular topic and give short highlight summaries. Other FDsys collections are also searchable on iPad (Figure 2.4).

Other Resources on FDsys

Highly recommended is *Browse Government Publications* at the top left of the main FDsys screen. This takes you to a page where you can sort government publications by *Collection, Committee, Date,* and *Government Author.* It is worth taking some time to become familiar with the *Collection* page. You'll see that each collection title shows the dates of coverage and links directly to the documents. At the top, you'll see a link to *Additional Government Publications.* This links to a variety of extra resources and is where you will find items such as selected hearings on the *Challenger Space Shuttle Accident,* records of *John F. Kennedy's Assassination,* and *Records of the Watergate Special Prosecution Force, 1971–1977.* At the bottom of the *Collection* page is a list of other resources that have been generated in partnership with federal depository libraries and other entities such as the Federal Reserve Bank of St. Louis. The GPO continues to seek new partnership opportunities and this list is bound to grow. In it you will find various sites of interest such as *Core Documents of our Democracy, Historic Government Publications from World War II, Historical Publications of the United States Commission*

Figure 2.5 GovInfo Beta site.

on Civil Rights, and *Information by Topic*. Keep in mind that occasionally links are no longer viable and the sites are undergoing changes. FDsys will be revamped and replaced by a new site called GovInfo sometime in 2017 (see Figure 2.5).

CONGRESS.GOV AND THOMAS

Sponsored by the **Library of Congress (LOC)** and named after Thomas Jefferson, **THOMAS** is being phased out and will eventually be completely replaced by **Congress.gov** in 2016. Both Congress.gov and its precursor THOMAS were developed specifically to track current and past legislation. THOMAS is the original, more text-based version of the site. Congress.gov is set up to be more flexible and appeal to users who have different information-gathering styles. Instead of a text-based presentation, Congress.gov provides nine separate video presentations that highlight the various stages of the legislative process. Students can also go to the *U.S. Founding Documents* link on Congress.gov and see the same primary resources accessed through Ben's Guide, but with more thorough coverage from the Library of Congress. As information slowly migrates from THOMAS to Congress.gov, Congress.gov often points to information still held in THOMAS. THOMAS is scheduled to retire by the close of 2016. However, until all the data migrate to Congress.gov, THOMAS will be available to the user.

Search with THOMAS

THOMAS was originally mandated by the 104th Congress to make federal legislative information freely available to the public. With this goal the site was brought online in 1995 (About THOMAS). It was originally used mostly by federal depository libraries and university students. With the proliferation of computers and now handheld devices, the ability of the public to access this information is significantly enhanced. Over the years consumer expectations of online materials have shifted radically, necessitating the changeover to the new version of THOMAS, **Congress.gov**.

URL: http://thomas.loc.gov/home/thomas.php
Grade Level: 9–12 with guidance/adult
Selected Coverage:

- Federal legislative information from 1989 through 113th Congress
- Congressional record—most from 101st Congress to 113th Congress
- Committee reports—104th to 113th Congress

- Presidential nominations
- Treaties
- Government resources: learning about the legislative process
- Teacher's guides

For the purposes of this book, the most useful links on THOMAS are the link to information on the THOMAS home page under the heading *Learn*, and the *For Teachers* link on the *About THOMAS* page. The *Learn* links that stand out for the educator are: *The Legislative Process, Supreme Court, Declaration of Independence, U.S. Constitution*, and *More Historical Documents*, which covers primary source materials from 1775 through 1870.

Under the *Legislative Process* link, the first two links, *How Our Laws Are Made* and *Enactment of a Law*, give very detailed, scaffolded explanations of the legislative process. The link to *Kids in the House—How Laws Are Made* takes you to a site hosted by the clerk of the House of Representatives that is kid friendly and divided by topic and age groups (*Young Learners, Grade School, Middle School, and High School*). Try choosing the age groups from the tabs at the top of the page and then select the topic, *How Laws Are Made*. If you click on the linked age groups in the list on the home page, you'll be taken to pages that are formatted somewhat differently and are less intuitive for the student. There is a *Teacher link* on the *Kids in the House* site as well. The other links from the Learn list at THOMAS are directed toward older students and adults. The *For Teachers* page accessed from the *About THOMAS* page has many more resources that will be useful for lesson planning with links to external sites that are suitable for kids.

Search with Congress.gov

Congress.gov, sponsored by the Library of Congress, will eventually fully replace the THOMAS site. It focuses on legislative information, providing a basic search at the top of the page and a link to an advanced search capability. The basic search allows the user to search by keyword or bill number. The default is to search current legislation, but there is a drop-down menu to choose all legislation, all sources or limit by five specific sources, *Members, Congressional Record, Committee Reports, Nomination*, and *Treaty Documents*.

URL: https://www.congress.gov/
Grade Level: Adult and 9–12 with adult supervision
Selected Coverage:

- Resources A–Z list
- House of Representatives—links for educators and students at top of the house.gov page
- Senate

- Audio and visual resources
- Learn about the legislative process—text and videos
- Teacher lesson plans
- Most-viewed bills
- Links to historical U.S. Founding documents (1774–1875)

After entering a key phrase in the main Congress.gov search box such as "health care," the user sees a page listing any legislation related to health care. To the left of the list, the user can limit by source, *Congressional Session, Bill Type, Status of Legislation, Subject/Policy Area, Chamber of Congress (House or Senate), Sponsors, Co-sponsors,* and *Party.* It is possible to select all categories under a source or choose specific ones. Clicking the plus (+) sign gives a comprehensive list of sources to choose from. For instance, if you wanted to see any health care bills that became law during the 113th Congress, you could set your limits to 113th Congress, *Status of Legislation/Became Law.* The next screen will show that 92 laws were made having something to do with health care, everything from the *Veterans Traumatic Brain Injury Care Improvement Act of 2014* to various appropriations acts. If you check the *within the results* box provided in the main search box and type in a new keyword such as "traumatic brain injury," you get five results of laws that mention traumatic brain injury somewhere in the text of the law. This full-text searching functionality is invaluable for research. Once you have chosen a particular law to read, by clicking on the bill number, in this case S2539, go to the page that shows the detailed information about the law and its progress through the legislative process. Students may want to look at the summary first to get an idea of what the law is about before diving into the full text. They can also discover who introduced the bill in the first place, who the sponsors and cosponsors were, and much more information about the process.

At the bottom of the Congress.gov main page under *Resources* you can link to *Teacher Lesson Plans* at the Library of Congress *Teachers* page. This site is discussed at length in Chapter 5.

APPS AND MOBILE SITES

We the People

We the People is an app available from the Library of Congress to download for iPhone or iPad. *We the People* is an authenticated mobile version of the *Constitution of the United States of America: Analysis and Interpretation.* Prepared by the Congressional Research Service, it contains a revised and updated version of the analysis, Senate Document 112–9. It is presented as PDF files that contain the following:

- Full text of the document
- Table of contents
- Clause-by-clause discussion of the entire Constitution
- All Supreme Court cases and selected historical documents relevant to its interpretation
- All federal, state, and local laws struck down by the Supreme Court and all cases where the Court overturned prior precedent
- Alerts to updates
- Table of cases and index

Congressional Record

The *Congressional Record* app from the Library of Congress provides access to the Congressional Record from January 1995 to the present. It is currently available for iPhone or iPad.

Other Apps for Congressional Information

My Congress: Although not one provided by the federal government, this app, by ObjectiveApps LLC, allows you to find members of Congress for your district by entering your zip code. Then you can link to their websites, find contact information, watch YouTube videos about their initiatives, and see their Twitter feeds. Until early 2016 there was also a link to the Sunlight Foundation's *Open Congress* page, where you could find details about bills each person has sponsored or co-sponsored, length of service, and committee memberships. *Open Congress* began redirecting users to *GovTrack* for this information in March of 2016. *GovTrack* is a site dedicated to government transparency that provides various types of data, including statistical analyses.

Congress is an app sponsored by the Sunlight Foundation: "A nonpartisan nonprofit that advocates for open government globally and uses technology to make government more accountable to all" (Sunlight, 2015).

The app allows the user to choose to engage in various activities such as:

- Follow Senators and Representatives.
- Sign up for notifications.
- Track progress of active bills.
- Find government hearings
- Follow congressional committee information.

The Sunlight Foundation also sponsors *Open States* to help users track state government (see Figure 2.6).

Figure 2.6   Highlighted App: Open States, created by the Sunlight Foundation. This app allows the user to follow information about state legislative process.

DISPLAYS AND PROGRAMS FOR YOUR LIBRARY

The types of displays that you can create about the federal government are limited only by your imagination. There are many resources available at various government websites to fulfill your needs. If you do an image search on Google using the phrase "how a bill becomes a law GPO," you'll find a GPO chart of the legislative process. If you are close to a federal depository library, the librarian there can probably provide you with handouts of the chart. Ask a local legislator to come and give a talk about both state and federal governments. Create a display of information about your favorite famous legislator. Offer a contest or drawing and ask questions about historical documents. One idea is to have a "Who Signed the Constitution" contest for the teen library. Ask who was the youngest or oldest signer and how old were they. This may necessitate some online searching on the students' part and can be a fascinating experience for them in conducting a search and evaluating the authenticity of the information they find. An interactive alternative would be to provide flash cards with various questions and answers to help them find the information (see Figure 2.7).

Figure 2.7 Constitution Day interactive display.

A simple display idea would be to have pictures and biographies of either state or national legislators. Get in touch with your closest FDLP library and ask if the librarian can come and share her expertise. Often, the librarian can also bring documents of interest, or target the presentation to a particular topic of interest at the time.

Given the ubiquitous nature of government information, you are more likely to find too much rather than too little. The way to control that is to think carefully about what it is that you would like to present to your patrons and then narrow it down to a manageable number of authentic sites. Focus on one government agency at a time or combine agencies with complimentary roles. An example of this would be the U.S. Citizenship and Immigration Services combined with the Department of Labor, the U.S. Equal Employment Opportunity Commission, and the state Department of Education. Migrants and immigrants inhabit a gray area where employment practices are concerned and would appreciate understanding their rights. They are also in need of information about how to provide education for their children. When you use your imagination you'll find that many government agencies overlap allowing for a multifaceted view of government services for your patrons.

REFERENCES

Library of Congress: THOMAS. "About THOMAS," accessed December 29, 2015, http://thomas.loc.gov/home/abt_thom.html

Sunlight Foundation. "Our Mission," accessed January 8, 2016, http://sunlightfoundation.com/about/

3

The Government and Education

The government is interested in education at all levels. Various government agencies produce materials online to support education that can be used to advantage by public and school librarians, teachers, and homeschoolers. Many of the education resources can be accessed as links from Ben's Guide. It is important to know what these sites offer in order to help parents who are homeschooling take advantage of the complex array of possibilities. It takes time to become familiar with a particular site, and each one has significant differences, strengths, and weaknesses.

EDUCATION RESOURCES FOR LIFELONG LEARNING

Every government agency can potentially put education at the heart of its mission and many do. However, there are specific education sites that are directed to the goal of helping parents and teachers make sense of the many resources available. Three of these are **Kids.gov** from the General Services Administration (GSA) and **EDSITEment** from the National Endowment for Humanities, and the **Department of Education** website. These three will be the focus of this chapter, although it will soon become apparent that each one of these sites is supported by the important work of other government agencies and that all are linked in a web of information that encompasses many different subjects and goals. Go to **USA .gov** and enter a search for "education resources" to see more possibilities and get a sense of the government information available from the various agencies that will be discussed in later chapters.

Start with Kids.gov

Kids.gov, developed by the GSA's Office of Citizen Services and Innovative Technologies, is a site that has been especially prepared to aid teachers and parents in connecting elementary and middle school children to government information resources. Closely linked with Ben's Guide, it goes beyond Ben's Guide's emphasis on the government and governmental process. Kids.gov takes a broader focus, showcasing resources from government agencies that can support teaching and learning at all levels of the curriculum in multiple subject areas.

URL: http://kids.usa.gov/
Grade Level: K–8 and educators/parents
Coverage:

- Art and music
- Government
- Health
- History
- Math
- Reading and writing
- Science
- Social studies
- Personal skills

Kids.gov includes interactive games, videos, lesson plans for teachers, and parent resources.

Kids.gov is divided into four main categories; *Kids* grades K–5, *Teens* grades 6–8, *Teachers*, and *Parents*. These can be found on tabs at the top of the home page. For the *Kids* and *Teens* pages, this is further subdivided into three subcategories, *Learn Stuff*, *Play Games*, and *Watch Videos*. This gives you a clue to the potential interactivity offered at this site. For instance, as mentioned in Chapter 2, by linking out to Kids.gov from Ben's Guide you can direct children to more information on the branches of government. Students are encouraged to download or order a poster showing the branches of the government and are cautioned to get parental permission first. The poster enhances their understanding with visuals as well as a short text explanation of the separation of powers and the specific roles of each branch in the governmental process. The poster is also useful for a library display aimed at this age group.

On the main Kids.gov page, no matter which of the three subcategories students choose, they can see more information by scrolling down the page and picking from a list of other options or by clicking on one of the picture options such as *Learn about Your State*, an interactive map that allows the students to choose their state and explore learning opportunities from a state-generated website. In the case of Oregon, this is provided by the *Oregon Blue Book* and creates an opportunity to learn facts or play games such as Oregon trivia. The quality of the material presented depends on the currency of the state sites. Occasionally a link doesn't work or leads to something that is not necessarily intended to be for students. Many states do have wonderful sites that are worth checking. If you see a site that is not working, contact your state representatives and ask that they encourage some effort in building a viable state site for education about state government. To give an example of the hit-and-miss quality of *Learn about Your State*, as of this viewing Tennessee connects to a county map with general information; DC connects to a more general information page; Alabama connects to an error page.

The *Fun Zone*, found at the bottom of the Kids.gov homepage, links back up to the second category shown at the top of the page, *Games*. Next to the *Fun Zone* link you'll find a "Question of the Week." Once students have answered the question, they are taken to a page that gives the correct answer and also shows other questions and answers to explore. Who knew that Thomas Edison invented a macaroni machine? This is just the type of trivia question that inquisitive children will latch onto and use to stump their friends.

There may be some links that redirect to dead ends such as the *World Map Game* that used to link to an interesting and interactive site with information about money and world economy from the Federal Reserve Bank. Although this site linked in June of 2015, it no longer links and may be in the process of revision. However, if you know what the source site is, in this case the Federal Reserve Bank of Cleveland, a quick look will show you that the resources are still available on the host agency's page. Choose the *Students* link on the Learning Center page (https://www.cleveland fed.org/en/learningcenter.aspx) to go to the Money Museum online activities. After accessing the World Map, older students can choose an advanced search to find other options for learning about the country by studying the images on the currency. As an example, in the advanced search students are given category options such as animals and nature. The student can then choose an animal or natural site and see which country it is in and see it portrayed on the bill. For Sweden the 100-kronor note features the naturalist Carl von Linn (Carl Linnaeus), who developed the classification system for plants and animals. On the reverse of the note is an illustration of a bee pollinating a flower. This is a great way for children to be learning at many levels at once and connecting with other cultures and their achievements.

It is worth taking the time to explore each site recommended by Kids .gov and note which ones work the best. When choosing from the listed category items, such as *Art and Music*, you'll be taken to another list of possibilities, many of which link to different government agencies such as the Smithsonian, the National Gallery of Art, or to other entities such as

PBS or the New York Philharmonic Kids Zone. One of the most interesting in the *Art and Music* category is the Smithsonian's *Latino Center's Kids Corner*, presented in both Spanish and English. When entering the site, choose one of the circles at the bottom and then click at the end of the gallery tunnel to engage with Latino art, music, storytelling, and culture. Choose the language once you are in the gallery.

Exercise and Eating Healthy features the USDA and CDC alongside the Smithsonian to help children learn the benefits of exercise and healthy food choices, some of which are illustrated in the USDA Farmers Market logo (see Figure 3.1); *Online Safety* highlights FBI and Federal Communications Commission (FCC) information and fascinating video clips from the National Science Foundation such as "Birth of the Internet"; and *Math* refers to the National Bureau of Standards as well as university and .com sites for information.

The *Watch Videos* option accesses government YouTube channels for many agencies, selected videos in both English and Spanish from PBS, as well as Peace Corps volunteers and professionals from all walks of life sharing their experiences and expertise.

Figure 3.1   USDA Farmers Market in Washington, D.C.

It won't take long to see that an exploration of Kids.gov introduces students and teachers to a broad range of government agencies that can be helpful at all stages of the educational process and well into adulthood no matter what a student's interests. An early introduction to this agency hierarchy is essential for student understanding and navigation of government information on a lifelong basis.

The Demise of Federal Resources for Educational Excellence (FREE)

It is unfortunate that the **Federal Resources for Educational Excellence (FREE)** features blog was retired as of June 2015 as this manuscript was in preparation. As stated on the Department of Education website, FREE was originally established in response to a memo from President Clinton in 1997 and was regularly updated until 2014 (Department of Education, FREE). Many liked the layout of the site and were impressed by the choices made to steer educators to digital teaching and learning resources. Features that were particularly notable were the *Primary Documents* link that pointed the user to primary source material ranging from presidential papers to documents related to the birth of the recording industry and the *U.S. Constitution Workshop* that brought together valuable teaching resources for instructing students about the Constitution and its relevance to U.S. history. One significant loss is the *FREE Features* page that highlighted learning opportunities and activities that could be adapted by librarians and teachers for interactive sessions with their patrons and students. With the demise of FREE, prompted by the emphasis on custom search tools such as Kids.gov, educators have lost a highly accessible resource. One can only ask, "What next?" Lack of funding and support for these kinds of educational tools calls into question the viability of relying on any electronic information, yet electronic information is continually touted as the wave of the future. Therefore it is essential that educators become familiar with what is available and be prepared to advocate long and hard for continued support or viable migration of the most valuable of these resources.

As of May 2016, the Department of Education page points former FREE users to Kids.gov and other discipline specific sites such as **EDSITEment** from the National Endowment for the Humanities, **Science.gov** from the National Technical Information Service, and **Smithsonian Kids**. All of these will be very useful for the educator, but they do not fully replace the nicely formatted, all-encompassing generalist collection of lesson plan information provided by FREE. Fortunately, the most recent rendition of the redirect page shows a list of the FREE Features with the links still maintained. These will most certainly migrate to another platform eventually.

EDSITEment

EDSITEment: The Best of the Humanities on the Web is an award-winning collaboration between the National Endowment for the Humanities and the National Trust for the Humanities that provides a variety of interactive resources gleaned from the Web for students. It offers the broad coverage of subject matter that made FREE attractive. It also includes access to **Closer Readings**, a blog directed to humanities in the classroom. This is updated regularly, gives insights on newly published literature and discussion of educational standards, and shares special tips for teachers and librarians.

A first look at the EDSITEment homepage gives the user a clear idea of the subject matter covered. At the top of the page there is a changing slide show and links to lesson plans for *Art and Culture*, *Foreign Language*, *History and Social Studies*, and *Literature and Language Arts*. There is a *Best of the Web* highlight section just below the fold featuring website material from other entities such as the American Bar Association. In the center of the page is a calendar of events featuring birth dates of famous writers and important literary and other historical dates, handy for teachers looking to find something on which to focus or a day to celebrate with their students. *NEH Connections* at the left of the page features a changing spectrum of specific curriculum of interest and Public Radio International (PRI) Series such as the *Afropop Worldwide* site that includes videos and podcasts for a multimedia approach to learning about African music. The **Closer Readings** blog can be accessed at the very bottom or the top right of the page at the green Blog tab. Next to the Blog link at the top right is also a link to *Humanities Online Magazine*, a treasure trove of articles on literature and culture published by NEH.

EDSITEment is divided into three main categories highlighted in red at the top of the page:

- Features
- Lesson Plans
- Student Resources

On the *Features* page it is possible to explore resources by *Type and Subject Area*. The types are categorized as *Monthly Feature*, *Specialty Reading Lists*, *Spotlight on the Classroom*, and *NEH Connections Teachers Guides*. It may be confusing for the user because it specifically states on the main page that you can find things by grade level, which is only occasionally true in the *Features* category once the user has chosen a subject area category and clicked on the "more" link in an individual resource. The subject area page then may allow for a choice between *Elementary*, *Middle School*, and *High School* resources as well as *Additional* or *About the Image*. The ability to limit by grade is a more reliable feature in the *Lesson Plans* search. Once in the *Browse* feature accessible under the subject area, it is possible to drop down the page and choose by age groups defined as K–2, 3–5, 6–8, and 9–12. All of this is accessed most easily by going to the Lesson Plan search by subject that is on the main page next to the slide show.

The *Student Resources* category allows for the grade-level search from the very top of the page. Here, the educator may choose *Grade Level, Subject Area,* and *Type* defined as one of three possibilities, *Interactive, Media,* and *Student Launchpad*. For instance, at a K–2 grade level for *Arts and Culture* using the *Interactive* type, the user gets two results, *The Roman World* and *A Trip to Wonderland: Sizing Up Alice*. The *Alice* resource sets up the problem of determining what Alice does in each situation she faces by giving answer choices for students to solve the problem. A sidebar on the right links to lesson plans for teaching Alice in Wonderland and related resources such as "The Nursery Alice," a beautifully illustrated digitized version of Alice from the University of Florida's Baldwin Library of Historical Children's Literature. The *Student LaunchPad* seems to be a shortcut to get to all of the various resources. At this viewing, the *Roman World* is not linking well but the lesson plan is viable. Each lesson plan includes a guiding question, learning objectives, prep materials for the activities, and a suggestion on how to access the activity. Occasionally there will be links to related websites.

As of May 2016, EDSITEment is advertising on the *Lesson Plans* page for writers to submit lesson plans, a great opportunity for teachers who are familiar with the Common Core to share their ideas and classroom successes. This is a wonderful site for teachers looking for ideas and needing an anchor for a lesson. It is easily navigable with a tasteful layout and provides access to text-based materials as well as multimedia and interactive resources.

Bring the Museum to the Student

One of the most exciting advantages of online access to information and the variety of formats possible is the opportunity to familiarize students with the myriad of resources available in our national museums. In the past, people who did not grow up in the nation's capital and who didn't take the time to visit Washington, D.C., for whatever reason missed out on a plethora of free resources provided by the Smithsonian Museum complex, a gem of our national heritage. Entry to these museums has historically been, and still is, free to the public. Now, because of online technology and the efforts of museum staff, students in remote parts of the country have the opportunity to see our national art, historical artifacts, and cultural objects through a virtual interface. This is an unprecedented opportunity for educators, librarians, and parents to bring the museum to the student that will ultimately inspire those same students to seek out opportunities to go to the actual museums and see for themselves. The Smithsonian has developed an impressive variety of apps and Web-accessible sites to foster education about their collections. They also promote interactive education about science, art, and humanities, and provide lesson plans through their Smithsonian Education site, the **Smithsonian Center for Learning and Digital Access**. This site is discussed in more detail in Chapter 4. Most of the resources are accessible on a desktop or laptop computer with appropriate software. There are also some materials available on iPhone, iPad, and Android apps.

Smithsonian X 3D

One of the newest Smithsonian products is the **Smithsonian X 3D Viewer** to access 3D imagery of unique objects in the collections. The Smithsonian makes both images and datasets available and, in an example of how this technology can be applied to the classroom, has created an ebook, *The Mind behind the Mask*, based on a 3D life mask of Abraham Lincoln. The ebook allows students to explore the facets of the life mask and alter it at will to see different light and texture effects. The ebook also contains a vidcast on how to create a 3D image of a friend using an iPhone camera and taking multiple images as a starting point. It includes primary sources about Lincoln and poses a question to students about who Lincoln really was and what made him tick. The ebook is currently accessible on Apple technology and there are other 3D images accessible through both Apple and Google technology. These resources create an enhanced learning experience that helps students explore important STEM concepts through the understanding of the application of 3D technology and also gives them a window into history through primary historical artifacts. The site, in beta testing in 2016, will continue to develop into a valuable resource for educators and is currently asking teachers for input about their own experiments with 3D technology in the classroom.

Vantage Point: The Contemporary Native Art Collection

URL: https://nmai.si.edu/vp/
Grade Level: K–12 and adult
Vantage Point is an older mobile site from the National Museum of the American Indian that can be used as a window into contemporary native art as well as a basis for cultural study. As part of the *Personal Memory*

and Identity section of the site, for the project called "In the Garden," students can watch a video of artist Marie Watt leading a sewing circle in the museum. A creative teacher might run with this idea and create a sewing circle in the classroom to express the values of the classroom. The students can experience both the process of decision making around expressing those values and the hands-on process of choosing materials and putting fabric together into a piece of art to hang on the wall for the year. The site also provides video and audio presentations highlighting the ideas behind the work of other Native American artists.

Infinity of Nations

URL: http://nmai.si.edu/exhibitions/infinityofnations/
Grade Level: K–12 and adult
Coverage:

- Native American history
- Native American art
- North and South American Indian art and culture
- Contemporary Native art

Sponsored by the Smithsonian National Museum of the American Indian in New York, the **Infinity of Nations** is a site devoted to Native American Art and culture. It provides video and imagery with audio description of nearly 700 Native American artifacts, including beadwork, clothing, and pottery from the collection of George Gustav Heye. Originally created as a guide to the museum collection, the Infinity of Nations app can be viewed on iOS devices. After choosing the Infinity of Nations Guide the viewer can choose from a variety of options and see the related artifacts. Students can zoom in to see more of the image, take different points of view, and listen or read commentaries on each object and the cultural meaning behind it. An introduction by Buffy Saint-Marie is included.

An enhanced version of the same information is viewable online at the Infinity of Nations website. Students can play the Infinity of Nations Culture Quest game at the website. Students choose from 10 different regions on the map of the Americas to access learning activities and gain badges for the completion of each section. For example, a student choosing the Northwest Coast region of North America participates in an activity to learn about the Kwakwaka´wakw natives of Vancouver Island. The student can listen to the correct pronunciation of the tribe's name and then go on to learn about the cedar headdress carved by Willie Seaweed, a high-ranking chief. Each yellow highlighted word in the simple text leads to a definition or voiced pronunciation of the unfamiliar word. The main activity is one in which the student learns to identify the animals depicted in the carved headdress. Once the student has made successful identification and completed the activity, learning about other animals and attributes of the headdress along the way, the badge is awarded. The student can then go on to a new activity for a different region.

Find Statistics at the Department of Education

It is important for all educators to have some experience navigating the **Department of Education** website. This is the government agency most involved with education on the national level. Also, it is important to be aware that there is an education department for each individual state. All government agencies gather statistics and the Department of Education provides statistics to help educators understand their regional demographics so they can better address the needs of those they serve. The *Department of Education Data* tab goes to a page that provides links to information from the **National Center for Education Statistics (NCES)**, the **What Works Clearinghouse** from the **Institute of Education Sciences (IES)**, the **Nation's Report Card** from **National Assessment of Educational Progress (NAEP)**, and the higher education datasets compiled by **DATA.gov**.

When looking for statistics remember that there is always some lag time from the gathering to the publishing of the data. In some cases the latest statistics given may be a year or more old. Some statistics are based on U.S. Census data that is gathered every 10 years or the American Community Survey (see Figure 3.2), a continuous survey of communities that compiles estimates on a yearly basis. All statistics from the American Community Survey of 2015 won't be published until late 2016 or early 2017.

National Center for Education Statistics (NCES)

URL: https://nces.ed.gov/
Grade Level: Older students and adults

The **National Center for Education Statistics (NCES)**, under the umbrella of the **Department of Education** and the **Institute of Education Sciences**, is the federal government agency responsible for gathering and analyzing the most comprehensive education statistics related to both the United States and other countries (National Center for Education Statistics, 2016). When visiting their site, the viewer will see a rolling slide show of statistics-related material. Click on any one of the slides to get the data or materials available. This can range from information on

How the American Community Survey Works for Your Community

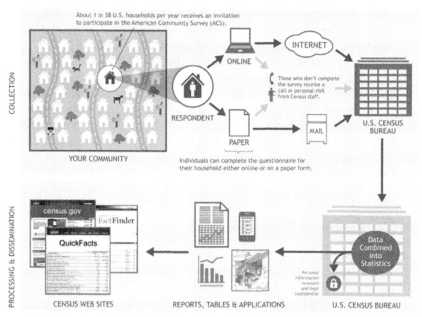

Figure 3.2   American Community Survey. Access full image at the U.S. Census Bureau website: https://www.census.gov/programs-surveys/acs/about/how-the-acs-works.html

Education Finance, School District Demographics, to a *College Navigator* to find the right college. Also included are *International Education Indicators,* the *Digest of Education Statistics,* and a link to the NCES *Kids Zone,* where students can explore practical and statistical information about their schools and community. The viewer can click on any of the slides as they flash by or go to the drop-down menu mentioned below to find a topic of interest. To see all the NCES linked information go to the very bottom right of the page and choose the sitemap. Check out the Most Viewed Sites category or target specific areas such as Elementary/Secondary Surveys. In the center of the NCES page the *What's New* section gives links to the latest statistical information on topics such as certification and qualification standards and school crime and safety. On the right side of the page, notice *The Condition of Education* link where you will find the latest reports for all levels of the curriculum. The fastest way to see a selection of options is to hover the cursor over the IES NCES logo at the top of the page. You'll see a drop-down list with a selection of topic tabs. For instance, the *Fast Facts* tab lists *Assessment, Early Childhood, Elementary, Library, Postsecondary and Beyond*, and *Resources*. It is possible to choose from this drop-down list or simply click on the main tab to bring up a page with the same list available. A typical fast fact that might be useful for the user is *Adult Literacy* under *Assessment*. A question is posed: What are the literacy levels of adults and how does the United States compare to other countries? A text *Response* is shown and below that is a statistical chart showing comparison data. Even though the data was compiled in 2013 to create the comparison, the most recent data it draws on are from 2012, reflecting some lag from collection to publication. Links to related tables from 2015 appear below the main comparison table. Over time these statistics could be compared to newer ones to give a picture of the state of adult literacy in the nation.

Institute of Education Sciences (IES)

URL: https://ies.ed.gov/

The **Institute of Education Sciences (IES)** is an independent, nonpartisan research arm of the Department of Education tasked with providing evidence-based research to inform educational policy and practice at the national level. The IES collects and analyzes statistics, conducts surveys, supports international assessments, and is responsible for compiling the *Nation's Report Card* (Institute of Education Statistics, 2016). There are many resources available from the IES homepage. Choose from the rolling slide show or access What's New at IES and *Featured Publications* at the top of the page For a quick snapshot of resources hover the cursor over the IES logo to see the drop-down list of resources. Most important for educators is the *For Researchers* tab that points to available data sets. Users can link to an array of data tools produced by the National Center for Education Statistics. Another useful choice is the NCES *Surveys and Programs*, which links to various assessments. Educators who are used to using the *International Data Explorer* can access international assessments and *International Activities Program* (IAP). The IAP provides a robust selection of comparisons of student achievement on the international level among primary, secondary, and adult learners. The *Featured* tab at the main IES page links to *Education Resource Information Center (ERIC)*, a digital library of education research essential to educators at all levels. The *Regional Educational Laboratory* links to research specific to regional and state education. The **Nation's Report Card** and **What Works Clearinghouse** also appear in the featured list.

Nation's Report Card

URL: http://www.nationsreportcard.gov/

The **Nation's Report Card** is produced by the **National Assessment of Educational Progress (NAEP)**. The NAEP has been a congressionally mandated project since 1969. Their stated goal is to "provide a common measure of student achievement" across states and participating urban districts (Nation's Report Card, 2015). To this end they survey students, teachers, and administrators using contextual questionnaires to glean information about their educational experience. On the Nation's Report Card main page there is a link to Data Tools that accesses a video tutorial on how to use the *NAEP Data Explorer (NDE)* and a downloadable *Quick Reference Guide*. The NAEP *Data Explorer* allows the user to view state comparisons by grade, subject, and student group. Alternatively, click on the boxes at right to view *MAIN NDE*, information on national trends in 10 subject areas. These are categorized as the *LTT NDE, Long Term Trends, HSTS NDE, High School Transcript Study,* or *NIES NDE, National Indian Education Study*. These links may change as new studies are implemented. Once on the *Data Explorer* page, it is possible to see *State and District Profiles* by choosing the relevant tabs at the top and choosing a state or district from the map or drop-down menu. Be patient: the initial page and subsequent selections can be slow to load due to all the graphic material provided. It is well worth the short wait.

What Works Clearinghouse (WWC)

URL: http://ies.ed.gov/ncee/wwc/

The **What Works Clearinghouse (WWC)** reviews the latest studies on education policies and teaching practices and gathers together what they consider to be the best of the research to make available for educators (What Works Clearinghouse, 2016). Users may first want to take a look at the *Quick Reviews*, located at the left-hand side of the page, to get an idea of the scope of the research and what is available under certain topics. A sample of what they term a *Quick Review Blast* is a short report on the "Association of a Full-Day vs Part-Day Preschool Intervention with School Readiness, Attendance, and Parent Involvement." The associated report gives a synopsis of what the study was about, what its findings were, and how the WWC rated it overall. The review includes a full citation for the report itself as well as information on media coverage of the report's findings. Readers can subscribe to *Quick Reviews* to receive emails about new studies. More reviews and reports on best practices can be downloaded at the *Single Studies Reviews* page and *Intervention Reports* linked pages.

Practice Guides address specific classroom problem-solving skills. Any and all reports can be selected by topic and type of report within the report pages or by clicking on *Publications and Products* and making selections from the drop-down boxes below the blue line on the next screen.

Library of Congress: Center for the Book

URL: http://www.read.gov/cfb/
Grade Level: K–12 and adult
Coverage:

- Reading lists
- Author webcasts
- Resources for teachers

Established by public law in 1977 the **Library of Congress Center for the Book** "promotes books, reading, literacy and libraries" (Library of Congress, 2015). Center for the Book affiliates operate in each of the 50 states. The website has a simple layout. On the left-hand side of the page the viewer can choose from *Books and Related Info* using the categories *Kids, Teens, Adults,* and *Educators and Parents.* The site provides suggested reading lists, including a separate category for classic books. It also links to author webcasts, featured books and authors, and resources for teaching reading. On each page it is possible to access the list of categories or choose specific resources at the left of the screen.

Materials from the Government Publishing Office (GPO) Bookstore

URL: https://bookstore.gpo.gov/
There are quite a few low-cost and free publications that you can order from the **GPO Bookstore** to enhance your collection, everything from ebooks to children's picture books. When searching the GPO Bookstore site, take a look at the *Award Winners* and *Featured New Books* on an occasional basis. Also, check by subject matter or agency to see what is available. The Department of Education published the book *Parent Power: Build the Bridge to Success* in both English and Spanish versions. This may be a good choice for your collection to help parents plan for their children's education. At $7.99 for the ebook version, it is well worth the investment. *Discovering the Underground Railroad Junior Ranger* is an affordable illustrated activity book produced by the **National Park Service** for children 5–12. The National Park Service promotes children's activities and is a

good agency to check for new materials. It is under the umbrella of the **Department of Interior**. Type "National Park Service" into the GPO Bookstore search box to see a comprehensive list of both adult and children's materials of interest.

Displays and Programs for Your Library

There are many ways that you can access government resources to create interesting displays for your library. Kids.gov is a good place to start to look for government information on many topics. Government websites with education links are also good for unexpected finds. Taking the time to browse websites of interest to you can yield interesting materials to file away for later. For example, one government site that could be useful for any display on the history of American Government is the **U.S. House of Representatives: History, Art and Archives**.

URL: http://history.house.gov/
Grade Level: 6–12 educator/librarian materials
Coverage:

- History of the House of Representatives
- Lesson Plans based on the publications *Black Americans in Congress*, *Women in Congress*, and *Hispanic Americans in Congress*
- Oral History videos of the House highlight dramatic moments in history

  - Declaration of war in 1941
  - 9/11

- House History Blog for Educators
- House Trivia and Fast Facts
- Education Fact Sheets
- Congressional Election Statistics—vote counts from federal election since 1920
- Book Request Form for beautiful editions of *Women in Congress, 1917–2006* and *Black Americans in Congress, 1774–2005*

The information outlined in this chapter provides you with an introduction to only a few sites that focus specifically on education resources for teachers, students, and parents. Subsequent chapters focus on specific subject areas, pinpointing government agencies that serve those areas. You'll find that as you read the individual chapters on science, the arts, and humanities, they refer back to some of the resources discussed in this chapter. As the GPO emphasizes digital information, agencies are revamping their websites and, in many cases, are including an education component at a higher level on the site so that educators will have an easier time finding the resources they need. Many are mapping lesson plans and activities to the Common Core State Standards. Most government sites also offer a feedback mechanism, giving teachers, librarians, parents, and students an opportunity to talk back. As you explore the information presented, don't hesitate to respond to the surveys and questionnaires. You and your students can make the difference!

REFERENCES

Department of Education, FREE. "About FREE," last modified June 19, 2015, http://www2.ed.gov/free/index.html

Institute of Education Statistics, "About Us," accessed May 18, 2016, http://ies.ed.gov/aboutus/

Library of Congress, Center for the Book. "About the Center," accessed July 26, 2015, http://www.read.gov/cfb/about.html

National Center for Education Statistics. "About Us," accessed May 18, 2015, http://nces.ed.gov/about/

Nation's Report Card. "About the Nation's Report Card," accessed July 25, 2015, http://www.nationsreportcard.gov/about.aspx

What Works Clearinghouse, "About the WCC," accessed May 18, 2016, http://ies.ed.gov/ncee/wwc/aboutus.aspx

4

The Government and Science

Government agencies such as the **Office of Science and Technical Information (OSTI)**, **United States Geological Survey (USGS)**, the **Smithsonian**, and the **National Aeronautics and Space Administration (NASA)** have wonderful services dedicated to educators, as well as information for the general public. Science resources are especially fine since they represent enlightened self-interest on the part of the government. When it comes to Science, Technology, Engineering and Math (STEM) education, it is important that the U.S. government maintain an edge in the race for the best, most advanced information concerning the earth and environment, the oceans, and outer space and technology. This is an area where we have been slipping over the years and now there is a push to rectify the decline. What better way to do that than by making sure that our young people receive every advantage that the best STEM education has to offer? These resources are invaluable for teachers, parents, and librarians. Some of them are conveniently made available online and through apps and mobile sites, loadable to both Android and iOS smartphones.

OPENING YOUNG MINDS TO SCIENTIFIC POSSIBILITY

The United States has historically had a strong science program and government agencies that work in the scientific fields are usually ahead of the curve when it comes to providing resources for education. NASA has always taken an educational role and has generously distributed sophisticated materials to schools and teachers. Now these have translated into online materials, apps, and mobile applications. A drawback is that now, instead of ordering a set of bookmarks or posters for the classroom from NASA, teachers have to print them out, which can be a problem in schools where funds are limited. This dependence on technology and the costs associated with printing hamper some users, while the immediate access to materials and the provision of multimedia resources can be a plus for others. The Office of Scientific and Technical Information (OSTI) is the Department of Energy's (DOE) library of research information and hosts **Science.gov**, a website dedicated to educational resources for grades K through adult. With the global output of scientific information, the Smithsonian is a valuable institution that especially emphasizes that perspective since it covers not only history and the arts but also the sciences within a growing group of museums that are available to the American public free of charge. This fabulous complex of museums at the National Mall in Washington, D.C., has pulled together some wonderful resources that make it possible to bring students into the museums virtually so that even the most distant communities can benefit. These three agencies and their contributions to science education are the focus of this chapter. Each plays a unique role in the educational process and has found a specific niche for its activities.

NASA: MORE THAN MEETS THE EYE

URL: http://www.nasa.gov/
Grade Level: K–12 and adult
Standards: National Science Education Standards, Common Core Standards, some specific state standards available on linked pages (e.g., Texas Instruments *Math Nspired* page)
Coverage:

- Science Careers
- Earth Science
- Science Education
- General Science
- Science History
- Life Science
- Mathematics
- Physical Science
- Space Science
- Resources in Spanish
- Technology

From the **NASA** home page, go to the *NASA AUDIENCES* tab at the top right to find information *For Educators*. At the right of the next screen find *Search Educational Resources* and choose to look at an *A–Z List of Publications*, an *A–Z List of Websites*, and *Education Resource Centers*. The publications link goes to a list where the user can click on a link to find the description of the publication or lesson plan. For instance under B, "Bag of Bones" links to a description of an activity to understand the concept of bone density. The user can download a PDF with the lesson plan, gather materials, and get started with the students. An alternative way to look for lesson plans and activities by topic is to go back to the main NASA *For Educators* page and choose the *Search Educational Resources* link at the left-hand side of the page. This takes you to a screen that has a keyword-prompted category search by grade level, type, and subject. If the teacher wants to teach a lesson about bone density to fifth graders, the same "Bag of Bones" activity can be obtained by entering "bone density" in the keyword search and then choosing *Grade Level:* 5–8, *Type:* Lesson Plan/Activity and *Subject:* General Science.

By hovering over the *MULTIMEDIA* link at the top of the *NASA Educational Resources* page, you can find videos, images, and *NASA TV*. Also under *Multimedia*, notice the *Interactive Features* link. This provides a list of interactive image files that may be interesting for students who want to know the inner workings of things. A curious student may enjoy clicking through a lesson such as "The Effects of Spaceflight on Our Bodies" to see images and read text explanations. Teachers can also subscribe to the *This Week at NASA* vidcasts and podcasts to get updates on what is happening at NASA.

At the left of the **NASA Education** page, there is a *For Students* link, where younger students can access the *NASA Kids Club*. At the top of the *Kids Club* page, students have the option to choose a skill level and choose games such as "Rocket Builder." This game gives children a lesson in following rudimentary plans and in seeing shapes and spatial relationships. As the child successfully builds each rocket a new rocket and new set of plans appears. Lower on the main *For Students* page more advanced students can view videos and play interactive games about the International Space Station (ISS) and the solar system. Younger students can download and print coloring sheets. Choose specific grade spreads to access materials suitable for a certain age group.

NASA provides a number of apps for viewing such as the NASA Visualization Explorer (see Figure 4.1). On the NASA homepage choose the *Downloads* tab, then *Apps*. There are apps listed by topic for iOS and Android technology.

NASA Visualization Explorer

NASA Visualization Explorer provides stories of space through photographs, animations, and visualizations, such as aerial maps and video materials. The user can download and save stories from the NASA

OBSERVING EL NIÑO

Explore how NASA will see this year's El Niño from the vantage of space.

Figure 4.1   Featured App: NASA Visualization Explorer. Observing El Niño.

Visualization Explorer for offline viewing on an iPhone or iPad. This is a rich collection of fascinating images supported by short text explanations of phenomena. The app is regularly updated and the user is alerted to new stories that are available. The Explorer offers access to six main categories of information; For example, the *Missions* category offers up-to-the-minute information on the NASA launch schedule, specific sighting opportunities for the ISS based on your location data, and a complete A–X (no Z in this one!) list of other mission-based information. The over 14,000 images include NASA's images of the day (IOTD), astronomy pictures of the day (APOD), and others. The *Videos* sections has materials that range from 20 seconds to over 5 minutes in length and highlight mission- and site-specific information alongside videos of an astronaut on Sesame Street who has brought back a rubber ducky or a cookie from space for a favorite Sesame Street puppet. NASA also has a Twitter feed that the user can access and a *Television* feed started in April of 2014 showing live views of the ISS. *News and Features* carries interesting articles about ongoing missions and scientific testing such as "Underwater NASA," an expedition into the depths of the ocean to prepare for future spacewalks. The *Featured* section is a favorite, with an image collection, interactive map, and text and image information about the solar system suitable for older students.

Comet Quest

Comet Quest (see Figure 4.2) is supported on newer iPhones and iPads and can be played on a desktop or laptop computer. When using the

Figure 4.2 Featured App: Comet Quest.

app, start at the *Learn More* link to retrieve basic illustrated text information about comets. Pay attention to the information about the Rosetta mission since the game is based on the mission goals and this will help students understand how to play. The students can go through the training module to find out how to deploy the lander, record discoveries, and transmit data back to earth while avoiding hazards in space. When students start playing the game they must remember a complicated series of moves to maintain a safe mission while gathering information. At the end of the game, students answer bonus questions related to the text information and can save their scores for future reference.

Space Place Prime

The animations on **Space Place Prime** are good combinations of image and text for early readers. The videos may work with older students but can be confusing and sometimes the presenter is less than exciting. However, there are monthly reports on special phenomena that will intrigue students who want to follow developments.

SCIENCE.GOV AND OSTI/DOE RESOURCES

URLs: http://www.osti.gov/home/ and http://www.science.gov/
Grade Level: K–12 and adult
Standards: Links to other agency sites that address National and Common Core Standards
Coverage: Extensive A–W list of science topics on the Science.gov Science Education page covering everything from agriculture to women in aviation

The **DOE** along with **OSTI** hosts **Science.gov**, a science discovery site for educators. The easiest way to get there is to simply type *www.science .gov* into your browser. If you would like to check out the OSTI homepage for other materials, which is well worth doing, you can access **Science.gov** from there by choosing the *A–Z Index* link at the top right of the OSTI main page and choosing S or scrolling the A–Z list. The new version of **Science.gov** is more of an index for educators than a site for students. It does have Trivia Challenge link at the top of the page that would be interesting for high school and possibly middle school-level students. The site is heavily text-based and offers no specific lesson plans. However, it provides a search by subject that leads to many links to government agencies and is helpful for older students to understand the agency hierarchy. It also offers a version in Spanish, **Ciencia .Science.gov**. **Science.gov Mobile** provides a keyword search by date range and the ability to view a list of participating databases and select a specific agency database. Some users may be familiar with **Science Lab** from OSTI, which was a much more student-centered portal. Unfortunately, that was retired in 2015 in an effort to streamline the search process through the new single-query access on the Science.gov page with mixed results.

The array of subjects and materials on **Science.gov** is immense, but there is no attempt to provide links to lesson plans or student-specific resources from the main page. One way to find instructional resources is to click on the Index link at the top of the main page and scroll down the index to *Resources for Kids, Parents, and Teachers*. This will take you to an A–Z list of possible resources, mostly linking out to other agencies such as the Library of Congress, U.S. Department of Agriculture (USDA), and the Department of Education. Many links go to affiliated educational sites such as the excellent *Natural Agriculture in the Classroom* link provided by the USDA. This particular site offers instructional materials from the National Agricultural Curriculum Literacy Matrix that align with State Standards and the Common Core. Unfortunately, some links from **Science.gov** lead to dead ends or caveats noting that the page no longer exists or had been discontinued because of lack of funding.

Nevertheless, the various agency-generated pages can be quite useful, and a careful study of these resources is worth the time it takes.

Energy.gov, one of the external links found at Science.gov, is another DOE site. On the Energy.gov homepage, choose the *Science &Innovation* tab at the top and *Science Education* in the drop-down list in order to find excellent videos for older students and adults, energy quick facts, and links to *Energy Kids* and *Energy Star Kids*, both geared toward primary students. There are also links to the *National Science Bowl* and an *Energy Action Checklist* in Spanish. At the bottom right of the page there is a link to *STEM Education Resources* from the Office of Economic Impact and Diversity. The resources are divided into two lists, *K–12 Resources* and *Middle School Resources*. One very robust site is "The Harnessed Atom." Directed to the middle school curriculum, it offers lesson plans, teacher presentations, and activities such as the game "Build an Atom" provided by the Oak Ridge Associated Universities.

The lesson here is that there is no shortage of resources, as long as you are willing to take the time to follow the links. The positive aspect of going to these sites from government pages is that they have been vetted for quality already and are doing legitimate scientific research and development. There are many rewards to be gleaned from a focused search of these government agency materials.

U.S. GEOLOGICAL SURVEY RESOURCES

URL: http://www.usgs.gov/
Grade Level: K–12, undergraduate, and adult
Standards: None
Coverage: A range of topics under the following main headings:

- Biology
- Geography
- Geology
- Water

The **U.S. Geological Survey (USGS)** also links directly to education resources for K–12 and undergraduate students from the *Education* tab on the homepage. These address various topics under the studies of biology, geography, geology, and water. As of this writing, these do not address Common Core Standards. Topic pages sometimes include complete teaching modules and/or student activities and occasionally include digital data or images. For instance, under *Biology/Ecosystems* there is a complete teacher's module with student activities included for "Lessons on the Lake: An Educator's Guide to the Pontchartrain Basin". This resource was originally published by the Lake Pontchartrain Basin Foundation. Under *Geography*, the USGS has created a guide for teachers, "27 Ideas for Teaching with Topographic Maps," which includes a teaching module, student activities, and digital data.

THE "SERIOUSLY AMAZING" SMITHSONIAN

For those who have not had the opportunity to live in Washington, D.C., for a period of time, or to grow up there with spontaneous access to the magnificent museums under the **Smithsonian** banner, it may seem an exaggeration that the Smithsonian has adopted *Seriously Amazing* as its trademark. However, most visitors discover quickly that a thorough examination of all the Smithsonian museums have to offer is an exploration that takes days to do it justice. With nineteen museums and galleries, nine research institutions, and the National Zoo, the Smithsonian is a seriously amazing wonder of the educational world. Originally founded in 1846 and funded by a bequest from the estate of James Smithson, a British scientist, the Smithsonian maintains a strong focus on education in science, history, and the arts (Smithsonian, 2015). Most recently added to the complex is the National Museum of African American History and Culture, opening in fall 2016. Plans are afoot for a museum of the American Latino and a women's history museum (United States, 2015). The Smithsonian also has affiliated with smaller museums throughout various communities in 45 states and offers an impressive collection of web materials, including apps and mobile sites that create a virtual world of information, accessible to all. In the future, these materials may entice young people to visit the nation's capital to see for themselves the wonders of the actual museums.

URL: http://www.si.edu/
Grade Level: K–12, undergraduate, and adult
Standards: National Standards, Common Core Standards K–12, and State Standards
Coverage:

- Art and music
- Health and PE
- Language arts
- Math
- Science

Navigating the Virtual Smithsonian

The Smithsonian is primarily about education as is apparent at their homepage. Front and center at the top of the Smithsonian homepage http://www.si.edu/ is a tab for *Educators* with a *Kids* tab right next to it. The *Educators* page has links to the *Smithsonian Center for Learning and Digital Access* and the *Smithsonian Science Education Center* that have an abundance of K–12 resources. The *Center for Learning and Digital Access* offers a portal for teachers, librarians, parents, and students to explore resources in several different disciplines, including science. The *Science Education Center* focuses on information on the *Smithsonian Science Academies for Teachers*, free ebooks, and curriculum aligned with the National Science Education Standards, Next Generation Science Standards, and the Common Core.

Center for Learning and Digital Access

This link opens up a colorful page that is divided into three levels of tab structure with further options to choose from drop-down menus. At the very top right-hand side of the page you can link to the appropriate audience by choosing *Educators, Families,* or *Students.* Within each of the subpages the second level of tabs allows the user to choose topics and resources specific to perceived need. Under *Educators,* for instance, the fourth tab is labeled *Lesson Plans,* whereas on the *Families* page fourth tab this choice becomes *Time Together,* and for *Students* it is called the *IdeaLab.* The third level of tabs at the center of the page is again focused on the intended audience. *Educators* can look for *Lesson Plans, Find Resources* by keyword, grade, and subject, and explore how the Smithsonian resources align with State Standards by keyword, grade, and subject. The *Educator and Families* page also features a *What's New* tab with the latest from the Smithsonian. On the *Students* page this becomes a *Know It All* tab, featuring things such as Sleepovers in the Natural History Museum, the American History Museum, and the National Portrait Gallery. The sleepovers have been offered since 2009 and operate during the summer from May through September offering a rewarding field trip opportunity.

Science Education Center

On the Science Education Center page, click through the slide show to find something of interest or go to the *Curriculum & Resources* tab at the top of the page. Under *Curriculum & Resources* choose resources by type, grade and topic. The *Games and Apps* link provides various games at the pre-K and primary level exploring animal habits and habitats, weather information, and insects, with a promise of more to come. Depending on the technology, the games may take some time to load. (Sometimes it helps to back out and try again.) The *My Generation Middle School Resources* provides lesson plans about *Electricity, Waves,* and *Information Transfer.* The *STC Secondary Teaching Resources,* also geared to middle school educators, suggests useful free apps from Carolina Biological Supply and has an alphabetical subject list linking out to information on other government agency sites such as the U.S. Department of Health and Human Services and educational sites such as Frank Oppenheimer's Exploratorium at http://www.exploratorium.edu/.

In September 2012 the Smithsonian started a Seriously Amazing campaign at their new website, seriouslyamazing.si.edu, to emphasize its role in asking and answering questions about anything and everything. The user can look for the SI-Q, find a question, and see the answer. Also users can submit responses to the Smithsonian on Twitter using the hashtag #seriouslyamazing.

Accessing Smithsonian Apps and Mobile Sites

The Smithsonian hosts a treasure trove of mobile sites and apps on its homepage. Choose *Connect* from the *Get Involved* drop-down at the top of the page to see the 36 available apps. If you choose *Explore* and go to the heading *Science and Technology* you'll find 266 different activities, games, apps and mobile sites directed to teachers and students. Some can be downloaded to smart devices and others are accessible on a computer. Most apps are available for iPhone; some include iPad and/or Android technology. These apps tend to be the most sophisticated apps offered by any government institution and are well worth viewing to study the content and find opportunities for interactivity in the classroom. These range from the "Shutterbugs Wiggle and Stomp," a pre-K, K–1 interactive game app through which children explore animal movement and habits, to the much more sophisticated interactive magazine app "Space Shuttle Era: Stories from 30 Years of Exploration." The "National Zoo" app shows webcams of animals in habitat, a fascinating viewing experience for any age group and a lesson in patience when it comes to waiting for eggs to hatch! This app also has a "Zooify Yourself" feature to allow the viewer to give animal features to any photograph of a friend or relative, a great pair-share activity in the classroom. Most apps are free, but the National Zoo app is priced at $1.99 on iOS devices.

Leafsnap (see Figure 4.3), produced in collaboration with Columbia University and the University of Maryland, is an app for sophisticated users who want to take the time to go out in the field, collect leaf specimens, and identify tree species. Currently it contains trees from the Northeastern United States but it is projected that it will eventually include all trees of the continental United States. The app uses visual recognition software to analyze photos taken by the user for identification purposes.

The Smithsonian gaming and app technology is more sophisticated than some other government games offered for free, as evidenced by the Titanoboa game an interesting app developed for a Smithsonian travelling exhibition. Titanoboa Lives, inspired by the original game, is an augmented

Figure 4.3   Featured App: Leafsnap. Reprinted with permission.

app found in the list. Many of the apps provided are exhibition specific and may not be available after a period of time.

The Titanoboa: Monster Snake game is very straightforward and will be fun for children in grades K and up with parental help at the younger ages. There are clear and concise instructions included. The tilt method of manipulating the snake to eat its food allows for fast and easy play, although it can make it easier for the snake to crash, a move that ends the game. Titanoboa Lives, the augmented app, comes with no instructions and for some it may be difficult to puzzle out. Point the smart device camera at the image of Titanoboa on another computer screen and wait patiently for the app to engage. Continue pointing the camera while going through the descriptive section. When the video is activated there is no longer a need to point the device at the other image. The video may hang up depending on your device and connection. If so, you may have to turn off the device and try again. Both applications are viewable on iPhone and Android devices. The Titanoboa game and the video can both be accessed on a regular computer from the Smithsonian site.

TAPPING THE AGENCY TREE

This chapter's four featured agencies are only a few of many that can be useful for a science curriculum. Others that are worth exploring are as follows:

United States Botanic Garden

URL: http://www.usbg.gov/
Grade Level: K–12

At the Botanic Garden website you can go to the *Learn* tab, choose *Educational Resources,* and link to the *Landscape for Life* learning resources that has detailed information about starting sustainable gardens wherever you live.

Environmental Protection Agency (EPA)

URL: http://www.epa.gov/
Grade Level: K–12

The EPA mobile site is an excellent entryway into EPA resources. Go to the A–Z list at the top of the EPA homepage, choose the letter E, and access environmental education resources that include lesson plans, videos and project ideas, games, quizzes, and other K–12 materials to use in the classroom or to inspire a library display. The EPA A–Z list also has a link to *Apps for the Environment,* where you will find resources to use with smart technology, such as the "Carbon Footprint" calculator for greenhouse gas emissions. Students can check their own households' carbon footprints by inputting the relevant information. This can also be found by going to the *Greenhouse Gas Emissions* page directly from the A–Z list. The "My Right to Know" app searches out industrial waste–producing businesses in the local neighborhood, affording students a chance to check up on the local environment.

United States Department of Agriculture

URL: http://www.usda.gov/wps/portal/usda/usdahome
Grade Level: K–12 and adult
Standards: National Standards and Common Core Standards

The U.S. Department of Agriculture (USDA) is another agency site worth exploring. Find the *Site Map* link at the top right of the page. Scroll down and click on the link for *Educators and Students.* Then choose *Agriculture in the Classroom* to access www.agclassroom.org. Bookmark this page for future use. The site provides links to a *Teacher Center* and a *Student Center.* Check out the *Curriculum Matrix* in the *Teacher Center* to find Common Core–associated lesson plans. Educators can also submit lesson plans to the matrix. There are lesson plans for early elementary (K–2), upper elementary (3–5), middle school grades (6–8), and high school grades (9–12). They cover health and nutrition, science, and social studies topics. Lesson plans can be searched by standards and/or content area as well as age level. Under the *Student Resources,* the *KidsZone* is a colorful site with information targeted to elementary level. Once you enter the *KidsZone,* click on *Exit the Intro* to see the various choices such as *State Ag Facts, Science Projects,* and *Virtual Tours. Teen Scene* will probably appeal mostly to middle school students. Here students can explore career options, find science fair project ideas, or watch a quirky animated video on integrated pest management.

Also under the *Student Resources* tab are *WebQuests,* a collaboration between the Missouri Farm Bureau and Missouri State University. The purpose of the site is to inform students about issues in agriculture. One of these created for the K–2 age group takes its name from the poem "Baa, baa black sheep." Some aspects of the site work well and others do not. The link to the virtual farm tour leads to a page that offers a free price quote for the tour. The user will need to have Adobe Flash to watch the associated videos. Even so, don't pass up the *WebQuests.* An especially interesting one is "Dust Bowl" created for 3rd to 5th grades, with links to wonderful photographs, historical information, and videos of oral history interviews with those who lived through the Great Depression.

United States Energy Information Administration: Energy Kids

URL: http://www.eia.gov/kids/
Grade Level: K–12
Energy Kids (http://www.eia.gov/kids/) is yet another place to look for lesson plans, games, and activities. This site won an Outstanding Website and Marketing Award from the Web Marketing Association in 2012. It also received two other awards in 2010 (Energy Kids, 2016). The site has a clean look with minimal links from the top page. It is divided into five main categories. There is an additional category just for teachers, access to online energy calculators, and a glossary.

Find education resources from other government agencies by using the *USA.gov A–Z Index of U.S. Government Agencies* mentioned in Chapter 1. Check the agency site map or index to see if the agency has a link to education resources of any kind. For example, the USDA lists *Educators and Students* as a link from its site map or A–Z Index. On the other hand, the Centers for Disease Control links to education materials from the A–Z Index at the top right of the homepage and National Institutes of Health links to *Science Education* resources under their *Research and Training* heading. A–Z Indexes seem to be more common than not, so the search process should be fairly straightforward in most cases; but it is good to be aware that anomalies exist.

DISPLAYS AND PROGRAMS FOR YOUR LIBRARY

Access to the resources from Science.gov, NASA, and the Smithsonian offers many opportunities to create exciting displays for your library. An example of a themed display would be something targeted to Women's History Month, highlighting famous women at NASA.

Women@NASA (http://women.nasa.gov/) features stories about women working at the facility. It also features a mentoring program for STEM education aimed at students around the country who can sign up to be mentored in their area of interest by a NASA employee through e-mail and chat. Display pictures and information about women at NASA. Show looping video that can be found under *Multimedia* resources on the main NASA homepage by typing in the keyword "women and STEM" (http://www.nasa.gov/education/womenstem/#.VNP1Hi4c6QA). Also there are video interviews of individual women scientists linked from the *Women@NASA* page. Many others are accessible from *NASA video gallery*: http://www.nasa.gov/multimedia/videogallery/#.VNP1wi4c6QA

Make Use of Mobile Technology

If you have iPads available in your library, consider inviting small groups of participants to a game day targeted to exploration of government apps such as Comet Quest, Space Place Prime, and Titanoboa: the Monster Snake. Comet Quest can also be played individually or in small groups on desktop or laptop computers. The instructions change slightly because of the lack of touchscreen technology (http://spaceplace.nasa .gov/comet-quest/en/). Another option is to encourage users to bring their own smart technology devices to the library for the event. For more sophisticated users, you might want to demonstrate the NASA Visualization Explorer, perhaps focusing on a particular research project about a planet or space mission.

More Virtual and Printable STEM Resources

Science.gov provides printable banners and bookmarks under the *Communications/Downloads* link, handy giveaways during a week of displays featuring government science resources.

The Smithsonian emphasizes the variety of virtual resources available. However if you link out to the museum pages from the Smithsonian homepage, you may find printable posters and other resources offered by the individual museums. For example you can attach the "How Things Fly" poster to a lesson plan from the Air and Space Museum.

If you are still searching for STEM resources, take a look at *Federal and External Stem Education Resources* from the Department of Energy Office of Economic Impact and Diversity (http://energy.gov/diversity/ federal-and-external-stem-education-resources). On this page you will find specialized resource for K–12 and undergraduate education as well as links for teachers. A great example is the external link to *Engineer Girl*, a site provided by the **National Academy of Engineering**. Here girls can get the biographies of women engineers and information on the profession, and ask questions about engineering. Include this information in a career day event in your library.

Each state also has STEM resource pages. If you go to USA.gov and do a keyword search for STEM education and include the name of your state, you'll be able to find out what is happening locally, which agency to contact and who you might be able to get in touch with to request help with STEM education. Informing yourself ahead of time about what is available will go a long way to prepare you for the student who comes to you looking for information on science. You may even be able to ask a speaker to come from within your state to offer a special program.

The list of departments that provide science education resources is varied, long, and full of government agency acronyms, NASA, NOAA, NIH, USGS, EPA, USDA, CDC, and more. This may seem like a complex array of materials and it is proof that U.S. government agencies have much to offer in the way of free information for educators, families, and students.

Educators and librarians can take advantage of the **What Works Clearinghouse (WWC)** from the U.S. Department of Education mentioned in Chapter 3. Go to the WWC and choose the *Topics in Education* tab to discover information on curriculum-based interventions and instructional techniques specific to science education. This information will help the discerning educator choose wisely from the many government sites available and inform feedback to the government agencies providing the lesson plans. We have already lost significant access to resources due to lack of funding, lack of interest and motivation, and, perhaps, low usage. As new resources continue to move to an online platform, usage and feedback mechanisms are even more important to establish patterns of engagement with the agencies that provide these free educational materials.

REFERENCES

Energy Kids, "Awards," accessed May 18, 2016, http://www.eia.gov/kids/news_awards.cfm

Smithsonian. "Our History," accessed December 29, 2015, http://www.si.edu/About/History

United States. *The State of the Smithsonian: Hearing before the Committee on House Administration*, 114th Cong. 3 (2015) (opening statement of Candice S. Miller, Chairman).

5

The Government and the Arts and Humanities

STEAM education is a concept of combining the arts with science and technology to give students a multifaceted experience of life. If we truly want to get back to the holistic view of education, the humanities figure into this equation as well, so perhaps SHTEAM can be the new acronym for the well-rounded liberal arts education of the future. The federal government is involved in the arts and humanities through government agencies such as the **Library of Congress**, the **Smithsonian** the **National Endowment for the Arts**, and the **National Endowment for the Humanities**. Librarians can help all patrons find out how the arts and humanities are promoted and supported by government agencies and where to find archived photos, audio, video, and literature, a broad spectrum of literary, visual, and performing arts materials for teaching and learning.

LIBRARY OF CONGRESS

URL: https://www.loc.gov/
Grade Level: K–12 and adult
The **Library of Congress (LOC)**, founded in 1800, is the nation's oldest cultural institution and is still the largest library in the world with over 160 million items in the physical collection and a mission to preserve millions of items each year. After the British burned the Capitol building in 1814 destroying the library's main collection of 3,000 volumes, Congress approved purchasing Thomas Jefferson's personal library of 6,487 books for $23,950. The Library of Congress is the main reference library for Congress and answered over 500,000 congressional questions in 2014 alone. It answered questions for close to half a million individuals in the same year. A quick look at the *About LOC Fascinating Facts* page will give you all this information and more (Library of Congress Fascinating Facts, 2015).

Library of Congress for the Classroom

URL: https://www.loc.gov/teachers/
Grade Level: K–12 teachers/teacher-moderated course materials for students
Standards: Common Core Standards and State Standards
Coverage:

- Classroom materials including free ebooks
- Historical primary source documents for the classroom
- Lesson plans mapped to Common Core Standards, State Content, and Organizations
- Citation information
- Professional development opportunities
- News and events on funding opportunities and grants
- Highlighted updates

The LOC website links to classroom materials and primary source professional development items for teachers from the *Education* tab on the homepage. Under the *Education* tab, the *Teachers* drop-down list is divided into four categories; *Teacher Resources, Lesson Plans, Primary Source Sets,* and *Professional Development.* At the left-hand side of the page under the general search box, all four categories give links back to the *Teachers* homepage or out to other information. *Lesson Plans* are listed from *A to Z* by *Topic* or by *Era.* These are based on primary resources available from the LOC. *Primary Source Sets* are also listed by topic alphabetically. After choosing a topic in *Primary Source Sets* such as the first one in the list, "Abraham Lincoln: Rise to National Prominence," the user is led to a page with a *Teacher's Guide* in PDF format, the ability to select by Common Core or State Content, and a variety of links to specific primary resource images from the LOC collection.

On the *Teachers Resources* and *Classroom Materials* pages it is also possible to search the site by both Common Core and State content. On the *Teachers Home* page under *Classroom Materials,* look for *Student Discovery Sets* (see Figure 5.1), a selection of free ebooks available using iOS technology. There is also a *Teaching with Primary Sources (TPS) Partners* page that links out to other programs at colleges and other educational entities in 14 of the 50 states such as Stanford University in California and the Collaborative for Educational Services in Massachusetts. The *TPS Program* also awards regional grants to organizations such as schools and libraries that incorporate *TPS* materials into their community professional development programs (Library of Congress Teaching with Primary Sources Partners, 2015). The *Using Primary Sources* link explains the importance of primary sources and gives suggestions on how to engage

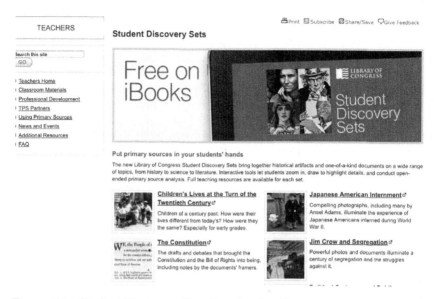

Figure 5.1 Student Discovery Sets. Reprinted with permission.

students with the materials provided and to assess their understanding of the exercise. *News and Events* highlights available grants, positions, and the latest lesson plans, among other things. The *Additional Resources* link connects teachers with resources from within the LOC as well as outside the LOC covering a variety of subject matter. Lastly, there is an *FAQ* page to familiarize users with the basics of the site and get them started on a quest for information.

Of course, the main LOC page is also worth exploring with image lead-ins to digital collections and a general search box that allows the user to choose resources by format. You may browse using the *Collection Highlights* links or choose from the *Topics* list. There are also featured videos and a *Today in History* link with fast facts about historical events. Don't overlook the apps provided by the Library of Congress found at the home page under *Explore and Discover*.

American Memory: Our Grandmother's Attic

URL: http://memory.loc.gov/ammem/index.html
Grade Level: Older children and adults
The Library of Congress, long known for its exhaustive collection of books and hard copy materials, has entered the 21st century as a late bloomer in the management of digital materials. Even so, the LOC site,

American Memory, is a vast and largely untapped array of resources of great use to the educational field. This national grandmother's attic functions as an accessible repository of old materials relevant to American history, culture, literature, and the arts. Many of the educational links mentioned earlier directly connect to American Memory collections. American Memory is such a rich resource that it is worth getting familiar with all it has to offer for future reference. From the homepage the user can go to the *Browse* tab at the top of the page to access browse by topic, by time period, by types of resources, or by place. There is also a link to an alphabetized list of all collections. Just recently, in an attempt at modernizing the site some collections have been migrated to other areas of the LOC site. That said, the streamlined look and feel of American Memory provides a comfortable portal to a variety of LOC resources. Once beyond the top page it may be worth getting lost in the links, like being lost in the stacks of a library, following the browse feature to surprises along the way.

There is a general search box at the top right of the American Memory homepage. For example, you may type the keyword "horses" in the search box, to get a list of materials in various formats. Click on the title of the item to view it. Notice that to the right are listed the titles of the collections that house these items. The items in this search result range from a transcription of a 1937 recording, "My Horses Ain't Hungry, They Won't Eat Your Hay," with an option to play the recording, to the text of a book by the famous Texas horse trainer Prof. J. S. Carroll. If you've never heard of Professor Carroll, it is no wonder since he hailed from Texas sometime in the 1800s. Perhaps you have more interest in an advertisement for horses created in 1847 as promotion for the horse and carriage business of Benjamin Bohrer, Georgetown, Washington, D.C. On the other hand if you are curious to know what kind of horses Abraham Lincoln might have favored, you'd be intrigued to know that in 1864 he received a letter from Mooney & Van Fleet offering a fine "pair of large red bays" for sale. In fact, the Abraham Lincoln papers contain quite a few references to horse buying and selling, not surprising since they were the main means of conveyance in a time of no cars. This bit of trivia would be fascinating for students. Of course it will be hard to comb through 5,000 references to horses. The *Help* box at the top of the homepage takes you to information on how to formulate your search, narrow it down, or zero in on a particular collection. The American Memory search only finds full text where the content of the item whether it be a book or a broadside is fully transcribed into searchable text.

The *List All Collections* link on the *Browse Collections* page is a good place to start to look for a specific interest. The collections are listed by subject and if you know a specific collection such as the *Variety Stage* collection, you can choose by title. If you choose the title of a collection from your list, you will be taken to the collection homepage, where you will find descriptions of the types of resources and the breadth and year span of the materials. *America Singing* is a unique collection of 19th-century American song sheets, dated between 1800 and the 1880s. Each of the song sheets can be seen in a digitized image. *American Variety Stage* is specific to vaudeville and popular entertainment between 1870 and 1920 and contains a range of different formats including 10 sound recordings and 61 motion pictures as well as playbills, programs, and play scripts. Once you are on the collection page, you can choose to search a subject or author list or choose the *American Variety Stage* link to see a description of the era and choose particular formats or subjects from tabs at the bottom of the page. Houdini rates his own separate page with 143 photographs and 29 other pieces of memorabilia. It is not always clear which link takes you to the actual digital objects. When in doubt use the *Browse* indexes on the collection page. Each takes you to a list of links to the images, motion pictures, or texts. As material migrates from American Memory to a larger, more modernized index of digital collections, much of this may change and collections should become more accessible in the future. Some collections have already disappeared from American Memory such as the *Architecture and Landscape* link from the *Subject* list. In this case the bolded link no longer works but the subcategories underneath do link to a new list of migrated collections in which you will find an *Architecture* link to Harvard University's School of Design. These are minor hiccups that may resolve before this book goes to press.

You'll notice that the American Memory homepage also features highlighted collections and *Today in History*, a daily link to historical events commemorated by the collection. At the middle of the page below *Collection Highlights* there is a *Teachers* link that leads back to the LOC *Teachers Resources* page that is detailed earlier in this chapter. Under Services at the top of the home page there is access to an *Ask a Librarian* email form as well as a *Chat with a Librarian* option that is available between two and four (Eastern Time) Monday through Friday, except federal holidays.

NATIONAL GALLERY OF ART

URL: http://www.nga.gov
Grade Level: K–12 teachers/teacher-moderated course materials for students
Standards: NAEA Standards for Visual Arts
Coverage:

- Classic and modern art
- Portraiture
- Teaching packets

- Themed lessons
- Posters
- Interactive apps

The **National Gallery of Art** was conceived by someone who worked in the halls of government, Andrew W. Mellon, a financier who was appointed Secretary of the Treasury by President Warren G. Harding. Mellon was an art collector and made an offer to President Franklin D. Roosevelt in 1936 to donate his art collection and funds for the building that eventually housed the National Gallery. The architect he chose was John Russell Pope, who conceived what is now known as the West Building. The East building was built much later when there was need for expansion. Even at the time, Mellon considered the educational function of the gallery as important. The art works are exhibited by period and national origin, and each room is decorated accordingly. As explained in the description on the website *About* page: "The Italian Renaissance galleries, for instance, have Italian travertine wainscot and hand-finished plaster walls and are detailed with base and door surround moldings and include built-in niches to display sculpture, while Dutch 17th-century galleries are finished with wood paneling to evoke original settings." Since its inception the National Gallery has accepted many other donated collections (National Gallery of Art, 2015).

At the National Gallery website access the *Education* tab at the top of the page to see the drop-down listing links for *Teachers, Families, Teens,* and *Adults.* The *Family, Teens,* and *Adults* tabs lead to information on gallery programs for those audiences and will be of interest to local users. The *Teachers* link is most useful if you are looking for education resources such as specialized teaching packets, posters, or downloadable art for the classroom. Near the bottom right of the screen on the *Teachers* page is a link to *Search Learning Resources,* where teachers and homeschooling parents can find items to borrow for a nine-month period. These include teacher packets, CDs, and DVDs. The resources can be browsed alphabetically or by type. The search box allows keyword searching by artist name or subject and format. Under the *Online Activities* link you'll find a link to **NGAKids Interactives** and *Lesson & Activities.* First, take a look at the *Lessons & Activities.* This leads to themed lesson plans for eight different units, spanning subjects from the basic *Elements of Art* to *Art and Ecology.* Each one presents multilayered lessons and indicates grade level (K–12). They all meet National Art Education Association (NAEA) Visual Arts curriculum standards. A lesson such as "Who Am I?: Self Portraits in Art and Writing" addresses both arts and humanities lessons, looking at the art and letters of Van Gogh and Gauguin and the paintings of Leyster, Siqueiros, and others to inspire self-reflection through visual art, poetry, and prose. The fifth- through eighth-grade curriculum is most thoroughly covered, addressed by seven out of the eight resources. No matter the grade level, this is a wonderful place to glean ideas and tailor the resources to a perceived need.

NGA Kids is an interactive site for children (K–12) that links from the *Teacher* page or directly from the *Education* link on the National Gallery homepage. These resources are equally intriguing for children and adults. The *NGA Kids Art Zone* interactives do require sophisticated software on an updated computer. However, there are others that work well on older devices, such as the story of Lizzy and Gordon exploring the Sculpture Garden, which was developed for 3- through 10-year-olds, or the *Adventures in Art* interactives that can be accessed by scrolling down and choosing them from the right of the screen. One example of the *Adventures in Art* collection is "Watson and the Shark." It focuses on a painting of that name by John Singleton Copley. The painting tells the true story of the rescue of a young boy, Brook Watson, from a shark attack. The virtual version of the story helps students visualize all the aspects of the rescue by allowing them to zoom in and out of the details of the painting. It was Brook Watson himself who commissioned the painting in 1778, 30 years after the event happened. He was able to tell Copley all the details of the attack so that he could execute a "moving" picture. The interactive successfully animates the painting in a way that children who've grown up as TV viewers can appreciate. Another of the paintings that is examined is Kandinsky's Improvisation #1 (Sea Battle), a lesson in color, shape, and line. The Kandinsky presentation finishes with an activity on using color to express emotion. As the use of digital resources expands, the National Gallery website will be a good place to look for updates.

The NGAKids App is a new app for iPad (see Figure 5.2) that won the Parent's Choice Silver Honor Award in 2015. Children are introduced to great works of art and learn about the creative process through nine different modules where they can manipulate famous paintings of various time periods and styles. They can also practice the art of collage and free drawing in the sketchbook, adjusting brush style, color,

Figure 5.2 NGAKids for iPad. © 2014 Board of Trustees, National Gallery of Art, Washington, D.C.

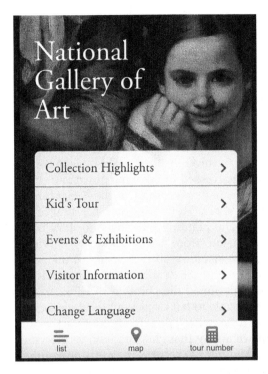

Figure 5.3   Your Art. © 2014 Board of Trustees, National Gallery of Art, Washington, D.C.

and transparency to produce their own unique digital paintings. They can save their work and share it with friends.

The Your Art app (Figure 5.3) is for more sophisticated users and would appeal to older students. It features over 130 paintings and sculptures from the 13th to the 19th centuries. The students can view the work, listen to commentary, and read text about the art. The app is available on both iOS and Android devices. It does take up a fair amount of space and may be slow to load on older devices. The *Kids Tour* on the app focuses on a smaller set of works that may appeal more to younger children.

A new and exciting offering from the National Gallery of Art is **NGA Online Editions**. This page provides resources for the more sophisticated users such as scholarly text entries by curators and art historians paired with images from the collection. The first of these focuses on Dutch paintings of the 17th century, with commentary by curator and art history professor Arthur K. Wheelock Jr. This page will appeal to researchers and college students.

SMITHSONIAN AND THE ARTS

As mentioned in Chapters 3 and Chapter 4, the **Smithsonian** once again lives up to its promise. It is an institution with the primary mission of education, giving teachers and students ample opportunities to explore the arts through the vast Smithsonian collections (see Figure 5.4). The Smithsonian boasts no less than eight museums devoted exclusively to art, seven in Washington, D.C., and one in New York City. All of the museums have active websites with links to educational information. DC locals

Figure 5.4   Smithsonian Art Museum Complex in Washington, D.C.

will be able to take advantage of programs for students offered in the *African Art Museum* (http://africa.si.edu/), the *American Art Museum* (http://americanart.si.edu/) and *Renwick Gallery* (http://renwick.americanart.si.edu/), the *Freer,* and the *Sackler Galleries* (http://www.asia.si.edu/) of Asian art. The *Hirshhorn Museum and Sculpture Garden* (http://hirshhorn.si.edu/collection/home/#collection=home) provides *ArtLab+*, a digital drop-in studio for local teens, and the *National Portrait Gallery* (http://npg.si.edu/) provides on-site opportunities as well as some virtual materials through its ***NPG in your Classroom*** digital newsletter. In New York City, the *Cooper Hewitt Design Museum* (http://www.cooperhewitt.org/) links to educator resources and lesson plans from its *Education* tab. These can be searched by keyword and sorted by subject and grade level. Each lesson plan correlates to Common Core Standards.

NATIONAL ENDOWMENT FOR THE ARTS

URL: https://www.arts.gov/
Grade Level: College and adult

The **National Endowment for the Arts (NEA)** is a granting institution that provides funding for project-based learning for K–12 students and educators' professional development based on a collective impact model established by the 2014 "Education Leaders Institute Alumni Summit Report." The report is available as a PDF download at the NEA site. One of the first places to look on this site is the *Publications* tab. Here the user will find the annual guide to the NEA, a downloadable PDF that provides information on grants available and funding deadlines. Grants are available at both the individual and institutional levels. The other option is to choose the *Grants* tab and search for available grants by *Grants for Organizations, Grants for Individuals,* and *Partnership Agreements.* Unless you are an individual artist looking for funding or an organization looking to fund a large art project, you had best look at the *Partnership Agreements* under the *State or Regional Partnership Grant Programs.* Section 3 under the *State Partnership Program* outlines goals for arts teaching and learning, for example, ***Poetry Out Loud*** activities. Go to the *Additional Information on Arts Education* link to see information on the possible components of a successful state art education program.

NATIONAL ENDOWMENT FOR THE HUMANITIES

The **National Endowment for the Humanities (NEH)** and the National Endowment for the Arts were both established by President Lyndon B. Johnson in 1965 to address the perceived need for the government to take an active role in supporting culture and the arts in equal measure to its already robust investment in science. Both entities are now 50 years old and are struggling to keep their place in an increasingly business-oriented, technology-driven world (National Endowment for the Humanities, 2015). Go to the *History* link on the *About* page at either site to read about the fascinating beginnings of these important institutions.

URL: http://www.neh.gov/
Grade Level: K–12 teachers/teacher-moderated course materials for students
Standards: Common Core Standards
Coverage:

- Language and literature
- Shakespeare
- Multicultural studies
- Grants for teachers
- Lesson plans from related sites

- PBS materials
- Lesson plan links

The National Endowment for the Humanities provides grants for museums, libraries, educational institutions, and individual scholars. In addition there are 56 humanities councils, one located in each of the states and in American Samoa, the District of Columbia, Guam, the Northern Mariana Islands, Puerto Rico, and the Virgin Islands. These are partially funded by federal grants from the NEH. Highlights on the NEH homepage include the scrolling slide show of the most recent offerings; *Explore the Humanities*, a changing display featuring NEH sponsored websites; and full text of *Humanities* magazine. Below the main *Magazine* link NEH offers featured articles of interest. A recent example is "How Did Cool Become Such a Big Deal?" an examination of the word "cool" and its cultural connotations. It is also possible to link to the magazine at the very top right of the NEH homepage. On the *Magazine* homepage, the user can see the latest issue or choose the back issues links at the top above the search box. The search box allows keyword searching of full text articles. Entering the keyword "horse" in the search box leads to "Vaquero: Genesis of the Texas Cowboy" side by side with "The Coney Island Exhibition That Captures Its Highs and Lows," the latter showing references to carousel horses and horsing around. When you are on the *Magazine* page you can choose the *Return to the main NEH site* link at upper left to return to the main NEH page. The *Events* link at the top right leads to a listing of NEH lectures, workshops, and exhibitions scheduled in different states, supported by NEH partner organizations.

Choose the *Divisions and Offices* link at the top of the main NEH homepage to find information about *Education Programs* at the top of the drop-down list at the left of the next screen. A favorite link under *Education Programs* is the *Featured Projects* and leads to interesting projects such as "Shakespeare on the Potomac," a summer institute for schoolteachers at the Folger Shakespeare Library that was offered in 2011. By following the links to the Folger page you can access lesson plans for teaching Shakespeare plays under *Teaching Modules*. These are mapped to the Common Core Standards. Often the partner sites such as the American Historical Association have an education or teaching and learning component that is worth looking into. Many of these are generated by NEH summer program grants for teachers and university professors. Look for *Attend an NEH summer program* in the drop-down if interested. Occasionally the links don't work because the project is finished and there is no viable link to an outside partner. There are also grant opportunities for projects under the program titled "Bridging

Cultures at Community Colleges" that focuses on the need for serious humanities teaching and learning at the community college level. Another NEH program to watch is the *Office of Digital Humanities*, bringing together the humanities and the technology aspects of STEM education under a common umbrella.

The *Explore* link at the top right of the homepage provides an opportunity to find out more about NEH-funded projects. If you scroll down to the bottom of the page you can choose *Explore All Projects* to go to a search screen that allows you to search by division and keyword. At the top of the main page a changing slide show gives a glimpse of the projects available such as **Afropop Worldwide**, a musical exploration of Africa, or the **Teenie Harris Archive** of photos of African American life in Pittsburgh 1935–1975. Others include the **Walt Whitman Archive, Chinese American Exclusion/Inclusion, Jewish Americans**, and **The War**, primary source firsthand accounts of World War II and lesson plans based on the Ken Burns documentary. The links lead to off-site resources such as the Public Broadcasting Service (PBS). Choose **The War** and you will go to the PBS page for Ken Burns' documentary. Look there for the *For Educators* link at the top of the page and you will be able to find lesson plans that include video clips from the series, a World War II timeline, a list of resources, and other valuable materials. The **Chinese American Exclusion/Inclusion** *View Project* link takes you to the New York Historical Society. Go to the *Education* link on this page to find *Curriculum* materials for the exhibition and a video conversation with Amy Chin, a New York arts consultant who shares memories of her early childhood living at her father's Chinese laundry. Another program is **Chasing Dreams: Baseball and Becoming American**. This one is sourced from the National Museum of Jewish History and examines the role of baseball among American minorities. Again there is a *For Educators* link to lesson plans based on the Common Core Standards. Each lesson is targeted to a specific K–12 age group. The actual exhibition was hosted at the National Museum of Jewish History in 2014 and then toured the country in 2015 and 2016. Many of these NEH-funded programs offer the option of small exhibitions or pop-up panel displays for libraries. There is a sizable fee for these services to cover the attendant costs.

The *Explore* page also links to **EDSITEment**, the most useful resource for educators at the NEH website. According to the *About* page EDSITEment was selected in 2010 as one of the top 25 websites by the American Association of School Librarians and is now part of the Smithsonian's Permanent Research Collection of Information Technology (EDSITEment, 2015). Chapter 3 gives a thorough description of EDSITEment.

One resource that appears both on the main NEH and the EDSITEment pages is **Picturing America**. The idea of this project was to bring masterpieces of American art into a classroom context to illuminate the history of ideas, aspirations, and ideals unique to the United States. The link from the *Lesson Plans* page in EDSITEment takes you to a list of 13 lesson plans available from the original *Picturing America* project, most of which target sixth- to eighth-grade levels. Scroll down below the lesson plans to see featured websites and a list of student resources. Each lesson plan in the initial list shows how many class periods would be needed for the lesson and provides worksheets to use in the classroom. It is important to remember that if there is difficulty returning to the list after choosing a lesson plan to view, it is possible to click on the *Picturing America* link under the lesson title to get back to the *Lesson Plans* page in EDSITEment. The lesson plan shows the appropriate grade level at the very top and there are four access tabs above the introductory text. The *Lesson* tab lists the guiding questions for the lesson, learning objectives, background materials, preparation instructions, and activities and also gives ideas of how to extend the lesson. The *Basics* tab covers the time required, the subject areas addressed, and the skills that are enhanced by the lesson. The authors of the lesson are listed at the bottom. The *Resources* tab gives links to the worksheets and any media that might be available such as the digitized photo of the work of art that inspired the lesson. Occasionally *Related Lessons* are listed under a fourth tab. The *Student Resources* links illuminate basics of composition and line in relation to the works of art. Some of the links are no longer viable, especially those provided for interactive materials.

Use the *Go to Website* link from the EDSITEment page to go to the comprehensive collection of materials offered at the *Picturing America* website. It is also possible to connect to the website from the NEH *Explore* page. *Picturing America* has educator resources available through a link to *Educators* at the bottom of the homepage. Once on the *Educators* page you can read about the goals of *Picturing America*, an initiative that was begun in 2007 and concluded in March of 2009 and was cosponsored by the American Library Association (Riechers, 2007). The most useful materials on the site are the *Resource Book* link that connects you with digital copies of a lesson plan guide written in English, Arabic, French, Spanish, or Portuguese; the *Head Start Resource Guide*; and the *Image Gallery* that contains digital reproductions of all the art pieces that were sent out to original recipients. These can be searched by *Image* or *Artist* and matched with the relevant lesson or viewed by *Theme*. There is also a link to a PowerPoint presentation of the artwork at the bottom of the page under *Resources/Images for Classroom*. The *Program FAQs* explain the original goals of the project to make tangible resources available to more than 56,000 schools and public libraries across the country, including 24" x 36" reproductions of the art works (Picturing America, 2016).

Finally, when you go back to the **Picturing America** homepage, look for the *Lesson Plans and More* link at the bottom left of the screen. This link leads to a list that includes some of the same lessons as well as others based on the original art works. Scroll down to link to the *Supplementary Visual Arts Lessons* for more advanced lessons targeted to high school students. **Picturing America** is a finite set of resources limited by the completion of the project and because of the tendency to link to outside entities, there are frustrating moments when the pages are no longer available or access is denied. Even so, these lesson plans can be a useful starting point for a creative lesson in history based on art or simply a creative lesson in art.

PROGRAMS AND DISPLAYS FOR YOUR LIBRARY

The Smithsonian emphasizes its virtual resources and helps the user find information at each of the museum sites. For instance the *Smithsonian National Postal Museum* site offers a lesson plan on the use of vacation postcards. Collect vacation postcards from friends and patrons to create a display about the post office and feature the postal museum. Introduce children to *Owney the Dog* through this same Smithsonian website. This affords an opportunity to create a program about dogs and how important they are in the lives of many people. This government information display can be part of a much bigger display highlighting books about dogs, facts about dogs, perhaps even visiting therapy dogs.

Since *Owney* was a postal dog, another option is to share activities from the *National Postal Museum*. Try out the game "The ABC's of Stamp Collecting" as part of your program. Ask a local stamp collector to come in and show part of a collection. Or try the "Help Keep Mail Safe" game. Using computers students can participate in small groups and collaborate to make decisions about what mail to trust as they go through the steps of the game. The game addresses fraud in snail mail as well as email.

As with many of the other resources in this book, access to and sophistication of electronic materials is constantly evolving. It is important to bookmark sites that interest you so that you can go back from time to time to look for new materials. Also, you'll find that you are limited by the technology that you currently have. Even so, the resources that you find will stimulate your thinking about creative ways to share new information about learning objects generated by the federal government. Since the materials are free, the more familiar you are with what is offered, the more apt you will be to find ways to use them in filling gaps in what you provide for your users.

REFERENCES

Library of Congress. "Fascinating Facts," accessed August 23, 2015, http://www.loc.gov/about/fascinating-facts/

Library of Congress. "Teaching with Primary Source Partners," accessed August 23, 2015, http://www.loc.gov/teachers/tpspartners/

National Endowment for the Arts. 2014. "Education Leaders Institute Alumni Summit Report," accessed May 19, 2016, https://www.arts.gov/publications/education-leaders-institute-alumni-summit-report

National Endowment for the Humanities. *EDSITEment.* "About EDSITEment," accessed September 24, 2015, http://edsitement.neh.gov/about

National Endowment for the Humanities. "How NEH Got Its Start," accessed December 26, 2015, http://www.neh.gov/about/history

National Gallery of Art. "About the Gallery," accessed September 24, 2015, http://www.nga.gov/content/ngaweb/about.html

Picturing America. "Program FAQs," accessed May 19, 2015, http://picturingamerica.neh.gov/about.php?subPage=about_faq

Riechers, Maggie. 2007. "Art and the American Story," *Humanities*, 28, no. 5, accessed May 18, 2016, http://www.neh.gov/humanities/2007/septemberoctober/feature/art-and-the-american-story

6

The Government and Numbers: The Census and Beyond

When people think about government statistics the **Census** is often what first comes to mind. The new Census site is somewhat confusing, yet can yield useful basic information for student papers at the university level. More advanced searching requires the help of a government documents librarian, geographer, statistician, or businessperson who is familiar with Census searching. The Census Bureau provides educational resources specifically targeted to K–12 students on a *Statistics in Schools* page. It is possible to use Census materials in creative ways to stimulate your students' thinking. Also, be aware that most government agencies collect and publish their own statistics often based on Census data. The Department of Education mentioned in Chapter 3 is an example. When looking for statistics, it is important to remember the power of an agency search.

DEMYSTIFYING THE CENSUS

URL: http://www.census.gov/
Grade Level: K–12
Standards: Common Core Standards for Math and UCLA National Standards for History
Coverage:

- Math and Statistics
- Statistical Analysis
- Historical Statistics
- Diagrams and Tables
- Data Visualization Infographics
- Historical Documents and Images

The **Census Bureau** is part of the **U.S. Department of Commerce** and is overseen by the Economic and Statistics Administration. The Census Bureau is in charge of gathering nationwide statistics about people and the economy. Every 10 years, the Census Bureau performs the Decennial Census of Population and Housing. The following basic information is a synopsis of what can be found on the Census Bureau's "What We Do" page.

The Decennial Census

The goal of the Decennial Census is to count every resident in the United States. The resulting statistics determine the number of congressional seats for each state through a process called redistricting. Redistricting takes place when population density changes, necessitating a change in congressional district boundaries. State legislators or state bipartisan commissions use Census data to make decisions on redistricting in their state. The Decennial Census along with the American Community Survey also informs federal government decisions on distribution of more than $400 billion worth of funding to the states.

The American Community Survey

The American Community Survey (ACS) is a second survey taken on a yearly basis to sample smaller segments of the nation for relevant data. One in 38 households are asked to take the survey. The information gleaned is more specific than the statistics in the Decennial Census. The ACS gathers information about educational attainment, occupations, home ownership, computer ownership and use of the Internet, and so on. The information gathered informs community decisions about placement of schools, hospitals, and emergency services as well as allocation of federal funding.

The Economic Census

The Economic Census is taken every five years to measure business and the economy in the United States. These statistics are important for the individual business owner as well as chambers of commerce all over the country. Government entities also use the information. This is the kind of information that would be useful to an entrepreneur or college business student who is drawing up a business plan.

The Census of Governments

The Census of Governments covers all local governments in the United States. These include states, counties, cities, townships, and school districts.

Figure 6.1   American Factfinder.

It also covers special districts such as water, fire, or library districts. Data about government organization and financing and employment are gathered by the survey every five years on years ending in 2 and 7 (U.S. Census Bureau, 2015).

American Factfinder (see Figure 6.1) is the online gateway to Census statistics. On the main Census page choose the *Data* tab at the top, hover over *Data Tools* and *Apps,* and then click on *American Factfinder* on the left side of the drop-down menu. If you have trouble with the drop-down, go ahead and click on the main tab to go to all selections.

Getting Your Feet Wet in an American Factfinder Search

URL: http://factfinder.census.gov/faces/nav/jsf/pages/index.xhtml

If you've never tried it before, searching for Census data can be daunting; so before you take this to your students, try it out yourself. The *Community Facts* box at the top of the American Factfinder page is a great place to start your search. Search for your city or town to see quick facts about the community. The biggest number you see when the page comes up is the population of the town. Then to the left you can choose the different topics such as age, education, and housing to see significant numbers in large digits showing the median age, the percentage of people with a high school degree or above, and so on. You can also click on the *Show All* button at the bottom of the topics list to see everything in a table. The table can be printed or saved.

Just this simple exercise in American Factfinder can give you an opportunity to compare two communities and learn more about how the Census works if you choose a different community to look at and make the comparison. The community you choose can be nearby or across the country. When you open each table from *Show All*, you'll see that much of the information comes from the ACS but some will be from the Decennial Census, some from the Census of Governments, and some from the Economic Census.

The *Guided Search* is the next place to go. Now that you have done a basic search and compared information about two communities, the *Guided Search* will help you build a comparison table. You can choose the same communities in the guided search and you'll get different information depending on what you choose. Click on the *Guided Search* under the *Community Facts* search box on the American Factfinder homepage. Then choose *Get Me Started*. There are five categories to choose from but your best bet on this first search is to choose from the top one, "I'm looking for information about people." Scroll down and click *Next*. On the next screen you have to choose from the list of topics under *People*. Try choosing *Age Group* and *Children*. This choice will be added to your search. Click *Next*. Notice that on the tabs at the top of the screen, you have chosen a topic and are ready to choose the geography. As a trial search, enter *Ashland Oregon*. In the case of Ashland, Oregon, there are two choices: *Ashland City* and *Ashland CCD Jackson County, Oregon*. CCD stands for a Census County Division that includes the town as well as outlying areas, thus a larger geographical area. Choose *Ashland City* and click *Go*. Now the first town has been added to your search. Now choose another town. In this case *Astoria Oregon* is used. Now you have a search that compares data for two different cities. Click the *Next* button. The next tab gives the opportunity to narrow the search by race or ethnic group. You can skip this step for the time being. Click *Skip this Step*. On the next screen you will see a list of tables. Not all tables will populate for lack of information for the data set. Choose *Profile of Population and General Housing Characteristics*. On the next screen you will see a table for the first city you chose showing total population and then the other characteristics. Change the geography in the box at the top to see the second city. Now you can compare the age groups of the two cities and other characteristics you are interested in.

Once you have perfected the search, show it to your students and have them take a look at how many teenagers are part of the population and the percentage of the whole. For instance, Astoria has very balanced numbers in the 5–19 age spread, whereas Ashland has a much larger number of teenagers. Even given the difference in the total population, with Astoria at 9,477 and Ashland at 20,078, it is clear that Ashland at 8.2 percent teenagers has a large teenage population in comparison to the 5.2 percent in Astoria. Your students will likely notice other interesting comparisons in the age spread.

Now, go back to the list of tables using the back button and choose *Profile of General Demographic Characteristics*. Point out to your students that this profile in which the two cities are lined up side by side depends on data from the 2000 Census, whereas the earlier one was from the 2010 Census. They will notice not only a difference in population but also an interesting difference in the percentage of teenagers.

Be sure to try this search beforehand to prepare for the class. If you complicate the search too much, you will get no data. The reason for this is that the Census elements have to coincide for the data to be extrapolated. For instance if the Geography you choose is too small, there may be no information available. In that case, you may have to opt for going from looking at the city level to looking at a county level. Playing around with the *Guided Search* is a great way to become familiar with the limits imposed. Eventually, if you are interested in more detailed searches, you may want to get help. At any time that you need more information go to the *FAQs* link at the top right of the main Census page to find out about citing maps and tables, explanations for the different Census summary files, and *Top Questions* concerning the Census. For your next step, guide your students through a search for their own town and help them interpret the data they see. If you don't have time to play with American Factfinder to get to know Census data, fortunately the Census Bureau has created a *Teacher* page just for you.

TEACHING STATISTICS WITH CENSUS EDUCATIONAL ACTIVITIES AND RESOURCES

Understanding the *Topics* page at the Census website helps you see the wide variety of applications of Census data. Choose *Education* under the *Topics* drop-down before exploring other aspects of the site. Here is where you can find targeted resources for educators. Choose *Education Main* in the white box or find a relevant topic in the blue field at the right of the topic page. On the *Education* page or from the drop-down on the topic page, click on *Teaching about Statistics* and you will see a page devoted to *Statistics in Schools*. As of this writing, this is a beta site and is still under construction. You can use the Census.gov link at the upper right above the search box to toggle back to the Census main page when you are finished. Tabs at the top of the *Statistics in Schools* page link to *Activities, Resources,* and *Standards.* The *Activities* page gives access to modules at the left of the screen for *Elementary School Math, Middle School Statistics,* and *High School Statistics.* Expand the *Elementary* and *Middle School* lists to see the relevant grade links. The *High School* module links to an *Interpreting Data* page. At the K–5 level, there are a variety of activities introducing students to the concepts of data and statistics. For the middle and high school levels, the Census Bureau has provided finished tables for students to analyze and interpret. Below the math links are history links. The activities included are mapped to the Common Core Standards for Math and the UCLA National Standards for History. Under the *Resources* tab you can access a variety of maps, tables, data tools, games, videos, and apps, among other things. The history resources vary from primary source documents such as the "The Census Act of 1790" to animated videos to data visualization resources. These resources overlap with some of the resources available on the main Census site that are described next.

Census Explorer, Infographics, and More

If you explore the various tabs at the top of the Census homepage, you may discover other resources for your students. A useful data visualization tool for your students is the *Census Explorer,* found at the main Census page under *Data/Data Tools and Apps.* On the *Census Explorer* page scroll down to choose *Census Explorer: Population Estimates Edition.* The *Census Explorer* maps the data so your students can get a visual picture of them as opposed to the table view. As of May, 2016 the data covers the 2000, 2010, and 2014 Census statistics and shows the population color-coded by the number of people per square mile. Click on the map to move it on the screen. Hover the mouse over the state to see the population for a particular year. Hover over the color codes at the bottom left to see the number of inhabitants per square mile.

You can also choose to show population by county and then hover over the county to see the numbers. Your other option is to create a visual of the 2000 and 2010 maps with the bubbles rather than colors. Again, the size of the bubble determines the population and you can adjust the size of the bubbles in the map using the *Bigger-Smaller* slider. By double-clicking on the bubble you can magnify the area of interest and see the populations of the counties. You can also use the plus or minus at the top right to change the magnification. This map can be shared on social media sites.

More classroom-friendly materials can be found if you go to the *Library* tab on the main Census page. Choose *Audio* from the drop-down to access *Profile America,* a daily one-minute broadcast highlighting historical information about statistics. The type of information you may hear varies. One day it might be the story of the development of shredded wheat as the oldest cereal product in the United States that gives statistics about modern-day cereal manufacture at the end of the segment. Another day you'll hear the story of the development of the transistor precursor to our modern-day electronics, or find out how many hot dogs Americans eat in the summertime. Broadcasts from the current month and the previous month are available for download. The broadcasts help show how statistics are used in everyday life and could be the basis for a weekly classroom trivia contest.

Stay on the *Audio* page and click on *Infographics* under *Library* at the left. Choose to see the statistics by clicking on the years 2012–2016. Each year shows different charts. The 2012 *Infographics* are a series of charts of historical comparisons between 1940 and 2010 on various statistics. There are also charts related to the different Census topics such as the number of foreign-born residents, measures of education, poverty, transportation alternatives by region, and more. The *Infographics* can help your students see the importance of statistics to understanding people in the United States and to learn about how priorities have changed over the years. For instance, if they look at the chart titled "1940–2010: How Has America Changed" and scroll down to look at "Racial and Ethnic Diversity," they'll see that the only races recorded in the Census in 1940 were "White, Black and Other." When they compare that to the 2010 chart, it is clear that the Census has changed over time and has started to collect much more detailed information on the racial makeup of the United States. This exercise can spark a discussion of issues around race, and why it is important to understand who we are collectively as a nation.

Stay on the *Infographics* page or go to the *Library* tab to choose *Videos*. Scroll down to *Education Videos*. The two videos by Eric Newburger, "Statistics in Schools: Answering the 3 Questions of Statistics Using a Picture," and "Statistics in Schools: Why Statistics?" are entertaining, short, and to the point in teaching a basic understanding of statistics to the middle school or high school audience. "Stats in Action: Park East High School" is an engaging presentation that follows a high school class learning about the statistics related to their local community in relation to the nation as a whole and the students' responses to this new knowledge. The video about the *Washington Post* Information Graphic Department is most accessible to older high school and college level students. It emphasizes the newspaper's mandate to tell a story using the statistics charting to draw people into the information. All of the videos have something to offer to broaden classroom discussion of the importance of statistics.

If you go to the *Newsroom* tab on the Census page, check out *Stats for Stories* and *Facts for Features* at the left of the *Newsroom* screen. This is a great resource for students who are interested in journalism and may be participating on a school newspaper or online blog or newsletter. The stories are taken from *Profile America* and highlight particular holidays, anniversaries, or memorable days in history such as "Women's Equality Day" or more frivolously, "National Ice Cream Day."

There's no harm in introducing older students to the Census site and turning them loose a little to see what they can find that interests them. Many students are very savvy about online information and they may discover things you hadn't seen. Every student should have a chance to see the *Population Clock* that shows the growing U.S. and world population in real time. Students can go right to *Quick Facts* from the top of the page, see the *Stat of the Day,* or try an *Easy Stats* search from the *Data* tab to discover the latest information from ACS about where they live. The more they get a hands-on experience in working with Census materials, the more likely they will be to continue to comprehend and use these valuable resources in college and in their future employment.

Beyond the Census—Agency-Generated Statistics

Remember the A–Z list of government agencies in Chapter 1, accessed from USA.gov? If you go to that list and pick an agency, you're likely to find that the agency provides statistical data unique to its mission. This is especially true of the larger government departments. Starting at A, check out the **United States Department of Agriculture (USDA)** website. Go the A–Z index on the USDA page in the upper right of the page under the search box. Go to D for Data and Statistics. On the next screen, you'll see data generated by the **Economic Research Service (ERS)** specific to agriculture, food safety, farm income, and other relevant issues. The **Foreign Agricultural Service (FAS)** provides statistics on trade, world production of agricultural products, U.S. exports, and so on. The **National Agricultural Statistics Service (NASS)** has *Quick Stats* on production and marketing data.

Obviously, with this many options, you'll have to be prepared to narrow your search to meet the needs of a particular topic in order to make these resources useful for your students. If you are studying about food safety or food safety comes up as an issue in the classroom exchange of ideas, then you may want to look at some of the statistics on food safety with your students. Another topic that is addressed well by USDA data is the environment and the use of natural resources. In that case, you can look at data given by the ERS at the link labeled *Natural Resources, Environment and Conservation.* Knowing these resources can help you tailor a lesson plan to include viable statistics from the federal government.

The letter B on the USA.gov A–Z agency list yields several agencies that are all about statistics. The **Bureau of Justice Statistics** is helpful for students interested in criminology or law enforcement as a career. The **Bureau of Labor Statistics** has a *Students* tab at the very top of the page that points to games and quizzes, classroom activities, and teachers' resources. The **Bureau of Transportation Statistics** addresses issues of energy and the environment as one of its subjects from a tab on the home screen.

Moving on to C, the **Centers for Disease Control (CDC)** lists datasets under the *More CDC Topics* tab. CDC statistics on foodborne illnesses will be useful in that food safety lesson. When you get to D, you'll see the list of most of the major government departments, from the USDA to the **Department of the Treasury**. Continue through the alphabet to find other appropriate agencies and see if they have useful data for the classroom. Not every agency supplies data as a direct link, but there is often data buried a few links down. For instance, at the **Department of Interior (DOI)** website, if you go to the *What We Do* tab and then click on *Climate Change*, you'll find *Scientific Research and Data Integration* as a choice on the right. The next page provides links to the **U.S. Geological Survey (USGS)**, another important government agency that is mapping the effects of climate change. If you linger here you will soon notice that the USGS site has an *Education* tab that points to K–12 and undergraduate resources of all types. Be careful, you may get lost in this wonderful page and forget where you started!

Now you've made the leap from one government agency to another and unearthed a gold mine of more free resources about biology, geography, and geology to spark new ideas for effective teaching. The USGS site is discussed in more detail in Chapter 4.

DATA.GOV

The **Data.gov** site is the federal government's home for open access data resource materials to support research on and design of data applications. The *Education* link under *Topics* accesses 300 datasets that might be useful to educators and those studying for a career in education. All are freely available. The data sets cover a wide range of education-related topics. Try keyword searching within the dataset page or scroll to get an idea of what is available.

Data.gov also points to data hosted by other government agencies that are involved with topics listed on the Data.gov *Topics* list. An example is the **Environmental Protection Agency's (EPA)** *EnviroAtlas*. The *EnviroAtlas* provides an interactive view of the benefits we derive from nature. Within the *EnviroAtlas* you'll find an *Eco-Health Relationship Browser* that functions like an interactive mind map of different attributes of the ecosystem and how these relate to human health. Use the video and text that gives an overview of the *Eco-Health Relationship Browser* to enable students to begin an exploration. Given the heavily text-based, albeit visual, format, this is more useful with high school or university students. One possible exercise is to have the students think about the relationship between the environment and human health and then create a mind map that makes connections between the two in their own everyday lives. Then go to the *Eco-Health Relationship Browser* to explore the topic more deeply and see the scientific evidence of the connection. The *EnviroAtlas* is an excellent example of several government agencies working together to create instructional materials for the public. In this case, the agencies involved are the EPA, the USGS, and the USDA.

There are several other examples of Data.gov topics that may be of use in the classroom. The Data.gov topic *Climate* also can be useful for environmental studies. Choose this topic, and you'll find the *U.S. Climate Resilience Tool Kit,* which gives students an opportunity to take positive steps toward discovering climate change solutions. Under the topic of *Agriculture* you can find the *Food Access Research Atlas,* which features an interactive map outlining food desert areas.

It takes time to explore available options on Data.gov. If you have an idea of what you are trying to find, try to pin down information by choosing a relevant topic and explore the topic area to save time. You can also go to the *Data* tab and search the datasets by keyword limiting by relevancy, ascending or descending order, popularity, and so on. The links may lead you to websites outside of Data.gov that are not government sites at all, such as Zillow, a real estate site that uses government data from the **Bureau of Housing Statistics**, the **Federal Housing Finance Agency**, and the **Census Bureau** to create its dataset.

Finally, under the *Applications* tab on Data.gov you can take a look at various applications such as the *Alternative Fueling Station Locator, College Affordability and Transparency Center, DataFerrett* from the U.S. Census Bureau, or the *AIRNow* mobile app from the EPA to track daily air quality. Many of your students have smart technology and might be interested in trying out some of the mobile sites available on the USA.gov Federal Mobile Apps Directory under the *Bureau of the Census* listing.

- America's Economy: Real-time updates on the state of the economy.
- Census Pop Quiz: Test yourself on Census statistics for the 50 states.
- dwellr: Share your living preferences with this app and find out the top 25 cities most suitable for your lifestyle.

DISPLAYS AND PROGRAMS FOR YOUR LIBRARY

When it comes to creating displays and programs for your library on statistics from the government, the sky is the limit. With the datasets available you have the ability to create maps and tables that reflect accurate information for whatever topic you choose. If you want to keep it simple, first create a display of Census *QuickFacts* about your community. Interview your patrons about what facts interest them and have them comment and share their comments on a bulletin board. Your display can be colorful if you include pictures that reflect truths about your community. This can be as simple as some of the faces of your community, young to very old. If you are not comfortable with sharing real photos, you can create color-coded paper cutouts to represent the percentage of different ages in your community, number of males and females, ethnic diversity, and so on If you are offering smart technology classes, you can encourage parents and children to download Census apps and play the Census Pop Quiz (See Figure 6.2).

Since many agencies give specific data related to their missions, you can create revolving displays of data for various state and federal government agencies that might be of interest to your patrons. When there is an important issue in the news, watch for data about the issue and include

Figure 6.2 Highlighted App: Census Pop Quiz.

data as a component of other displays related to your community needs. Data sets make a great visual display when you use colorful maps and pie charts. This type of display draws the eye and will help your patrons focus their minds on the issues at hand. Consider having a changeable display of numbers showing the U.S. or world population. The main U.S. Census page updates these numbers constantly on the Population Clock. Map the ethnic diversity of your town or city to spark a conversation on diversity and inclusion.

Display *QuickFacts* for your community gleaned from the *Community Facts* search: Manhattan Borough Snapshot for 2010 Census—Racial and Hispanic or Latino Origin 2010

1,585,873 total population
911,073 White 57.4 %
246,687 Black or African American 15.6 %
8,669 American Indian and Alaska Native .5 %
179,552 Asian 11.3 %
403,577 Hispanic or Latino 25.4 %

Spark ideas by presenting Eric Newburger's five-minute video, which can be found at the Census *Education* page. His premise is that you can take a picture generated by statistical data to answer three major questions about just about anything: "How big is it?" "What difference does it make?" and "Are you sure that it's not just dumb luck?" He shows how a doctor figured out what caused the London cholera epidemic of 1854 by mapping the area where the worst cases occurred, interviewing the populace and pinpointing the anomalies. This short video is engaging, humorous, and streamlined to show the importance of statistical data to the solution of a life and death problem.

GENERAL STATISTICS

Students must learn from the start that government statistics, both national and international, will help them at all levels of their education. The government has a vested interest in gathering and disseminating statistical information. In the United States, accurate statistics are essential to the government for decision making. The fairly recent Web availability of statistics has promoted more use by both print and television journalists. At the same time, when students read a newspaper or magazine article or hear statistics quoted on TV or radio, they should know that these are suspect, depending on how they've been interpreted for the report. It is always important to check the statistics at the original government source if possible. FDLP librarians can be very helpful in this endeavor since it is often difficult to interpret statistics out of context. There are also print and electronic sources available at the nearest university or public library such as the *Statistical Abstract of the United States*. This resource, formerly a government publication, now published by a private publisher, is essential for anyone looking for basic statistics covering many areas of interest.

The *World Factbook*, originally only published in paper, is now available to anyone online in its most recent iteration through the **Central Intelligence Agency (CIA)** website. Go to the website, choose the *Library* tab, and click on *Publications*. On the next page choose *View the World Factbook*. Search for individual country information by using the drop down menu at the upper right of the page. Each country entry contains basic statistical information for *Geography; Population; Economy; Energy; Communication; Transportation;* and *the Military*. There is also a *Guide to Country Comparisons* linked from the *World Factbook* main page that aggregates the statistical data in each category for all countries. Students can download the data or look for specific countries pertaining to an assignment. For paper copies of older editions, check in your closest public or university library. Students will find it fascinating to see how statistics have changed over time.

The knowledge of how to use statistics in research is essential to students in both high school and college programs. The study of statistics reinforces students' quantitative literacy. Once they graduate, individuals who understand the importance of statistics and their applications will be able to apply this knowledge usefully in a variety of occupations. There is no question that there are significant reasons to apply statistical information to the professions in business, science, technology, economics, political science, and the arts. Clearly, knowledge of government-generated statistical tools creates informed, employable citizens.

REFERENCE

U.S. Census Bureau. "What We Do," accessed December 30, 2015, http:// www.census.gov/about/what.html

7

The Government and Money

Quantitative literacy is an essential component of any student's education, and is just now receiving more attention from educational institutions and the government. Students who are unable to understand how to use graphs, calculators, and data sets are handicapped when they look for employment or try to function in the real world. Often understanding quantitative concepts starts with a basic understanding of finance. Financial literacy is not a lesson in how to write checks the way it used to be. Today few citizens write checks. The world has moved from hard currency to plastic to the Cloud in a single generation. Parents are trying to catch up to the shift themselves, and sometimes are unable to provide sound advice or instruction. Young adults are eagerly plunging into the market economy, sometimes ill prepared for its realities. By the time they are ready for college, most have at least one credit card and many are taking on significant student debt. Some are already entrepreneurs, promoting themselves on social networks. They buy their daily cup of coffee with a swipe of a smart phone. Young people also face the complicated task of understanding debt and tax obligations. They must learn early to protect themselves from identity theft as they navigate the nebulous domain of online finances. Fostering an early education about money and finance is essential to our children's future welfare. There are several federal government agencies that deal directly with these issues and provide information targeted to children and young adults. The U.S. Treasury website it a good place to start.

THE U.S. DEPARTMENT OF THE TREASURY

The **U.S. Department of the Treasury** is charged with maintaining a strong economy and promoting favorable conditions for job opportunity and growth. It also protects the security of our nation's finances (U.S. Department of the Treasury, 2016).

URL: https://www.treasury.gov
Grade Level: K–12, undergraduate, and adult
Coverage:

- Coins
- Currency
- Money math
- Personal finance
- Lesson plans

A link for *Students and Teachers* appears on the Treasury homepage just below the scrolling slide show. Clicking the link brings up a list of options varying from lesson plans to research for a specific topic. There are also links to *Common Questions*. For example, the question, "When was the Treasury Department established and how has it grown?" is answered on the *History* page with a short overview of the establishment of the Treasury. It starts with the Continental Congress's mandate to finance the revolutionary war. It takes a couple of extra clicks on history links to get to the full story. Another way to find this is to go to the *About* tab at the top of the U.S. Treasury homepage and choose *History* from the drop-down list. After trying this out, go back to the drop-down list at the left to find *Education*. From the list at the left of the next screen, choose *KidsZone*. Down the center of the next screen you'll see a list of links, the most important of which are the *U.S. Mint* and the *Bureau of Engraving and Printing*. Also, if you look to the left on any of the Education screens at the Treasury page, you'll find *KidsZone, Lesson Plans for Teachers* and *History* links. Several sub-agencies provide lesson plans: the *U.S. Mint*, the *Bureau of Engraving and Printing*, the *Bureau of Public Debt,* and more. Use these links or go directly to the website for each agency and check their education links. You may also find that you've already been to some of these sites if you tried the *Ben's Guide* or *Kids.gov* searches mentioned in earlier chapters.

The U.S. Mint

If you have ever been a coin collector even at an amateur level, you will be somewhat familiar with the **U.S. Mint**. Established in 1792, the U.S. Mint is an operating bureau of the Treasury Department in charge of the production of the national coinage. There are six locations in the United States where coins are produced: Washington, D.C.; Philadelphia, Pennsylvania; West Point, New York; Denver, Colorado; San Francisco,

California; and one we all know from Hollywood movie lore, Fort Knox, Kentucky (U.S. Mint, 2016).

> **URL:** http://www.usmint.gov
> **Grade Level:** K–12 and adult
> **Standards:** Common Core Language Arts Standards and National Social Studies Standards
> **Coverage:**
>
> - Images and explanations of U.S. coinage
> - Historical Primary Source documents and images for the classroom
> - Lesson plans associated with Common Core and/or National Standards
> - "Let's Make Cents" Newsletter with updated information
> - Games
> - Virtual tour of coin production

On the U.S. Mint homepage, click on the *Learn* tab and on the next screen, choose the *For Educators* link at the left of the screen. On the next screen you will see a colorful changing slide show highlighting particular coins or lessons. Below the slide show, you can find a link to the *Hip Pocket Change* map of the U.S. Mint facility locations. You can also see "Coin Curricula" link and a link to the "Lessons That Make Cents" newsletter. To the left you can access links to lesson plans, activities that include games and class gadgets, financial literacy materials, and more.

You can search lesson plans by *Grade Level, Subject Area, Coin Type,* and *Coin Program.* For example, if you search for *Grade Level* 12 and *Subject*, economics, without any other limits, you will find "You Can Bank On It," a single lesson plan about the purpose and function of the Federal Reserve. Each lesson plan defaults to a summary of the lesson. Use the tabs at the top of the summary to find out how to prepare the lesson, see steps for teaching, and find extra activities to extend the lesson. Some lesson plans include worksheets and basic assessment rubrics. Any association with Common Core or National Standards is also noted. In the example cited earlier, under the *Prepare* tab, there are links to definitions of terms and to a PDF file worksheet that lays out the lesson and specifies the associated national standards. An economics lesson for the sixth-grade level, *The Value of Exchange*, aligns with both Common Core Language Arts standards and National Standards for Social Studies. Each lesson is rated and you have the opportunity to rate the lesson yourself.

Try another search for *Grade Level* 3 and *Subject*, language arts. If you leave out any other limits, you will receive 82 lesson plans. If you limit to a particular coin such as the quarter, you will narrow your results. In the list of 61 results for the quarter you'll find that the second lesson is called "A Day in the Life," and is specific to the way of life of Civil War soldiers. This lesson plan includes worksheets and a project rubric under the *Prepare* tab and associates the lesson with Common Core Language Arts Standards. Two of the links to materials from the *National Park Service*, such as maps and historical information, may not be viable either because of problems with the site or ongoing technological changes undertaken by the agency. Have patience and follow the leads you find. You may have to check the URL given and shorten the URL to the basic stem to find what you need.

If www.nps.gov/history/museum/exhibits/vick/index.html is not working, you can back off the URL to www.nps.gov and try finding what you want by searching the National Park Service site for educational materials. By this time, your familiarity with the different government agencies and the ubiquitous acronyms for them will aid you in identifying who has the resources you need. This particular lesson is based on the set of 2011 quarters "America the Beautiful." You'll need to download images of the quarters under *Coin Programs* at the top left of the *Lesson Plans* page on the U.S. Mint page. If you find this or any other aspects of the site difficult, take advantage of the online chat option to ask questions. You can also email a question. Click on the *Customer Service* tab at the top right. The chat and email options are available at all government agency homepages and can save you a lot of time.

In the case of the aforementioned lesson, go to the America the Beautiful Quarters under *Coin Programs*, scroll down to find the 2011 sets, and choose the *Vicksburg* or *Gettysburg* sets. Choose the alternate view of the coin and drag left to view the image. Right-click and save on a PC or drag the view to a Mac desktop to save the image. Then you will be able to print out the image and use it in a Power Point or Prezi or some other presentation software program. Another option is to display it on your computer screen in a larger size. The National Parks Museum site will have details of the battle and more images to enhance the lesson (https://www.nps .gov/museum/exhibits/vick/index.html). You can prepare students early before the lesson to inspire them to save quarters and see if they can find and bring in an actual 2011 coin with the requisite image. As they start collecting they will begin to notice some of the other images of American history and culture and be encouraged to find out what they are by looking at the U.S. Mint website. Students can learn to look for the mint designation, indicating where the coin originated: P for Philadelphia, D for Denver, and S for San Francisco. On newer quarters this appears at the right side of the face of the coin under the words "In God We Trust."

There is much more of educational value at the U.S. Mint website. Older students may be interested to learn about the artists who develop the images for the coins. Some others will want to learn about collecting at the *Collecting Basics* link. The *For Kids* link goes to the *Hip Pocket Change* site, where younger students can explore, play games, and learn at their own pace. *How Coins Are Made* is a fascinating exploration of the minting process with a virtual tour to familiarize students with the steps in coin production as well as the history behind it. There is also a step-by-step text and animation of the process below the virtual tour link. For older students, the *History* link leads to the U.S. Mint *Historical Archive* of primary source materials about legislation, coin images, and more. The *History* page *Newsroom Image* link allows users to download high-resolution images of selected coins and medals both circulating and non-circulating. When you scroll down the *History* page, you will see links to browse the *Archive*. The *Images* link takes you to a page that defaults to a name search. However you can choose to browse by *Type (circulating and non-circulating), Denomination, Production Facility,* or *Designers*. On the *Documents* page you can browse by *Description, Type, Notes,* and *Year*. Finally, you can browse the whole collection, both *Images and Documents,* using a list view or thumbnail view of the collection. The U.S. Mint has quite a bit to offer that creates an engaging learning experience for people of all ages. It is well worth the time it takes to become familiar with the materials. As with any other government agency, knowing of the existence of these targeted resources and checking the site on a regular basis gives you plenty of options to enhance your lesson planning and engage student interest.

The Bureau of Engraving and Printing (BEP)

The **Bureau of Engraving and Printing** (**BEP**) is the Treasury operating bureau in charge of producing paper money.

> **URL:** http://www.moneyfactory.gov/home.html
> **Grade Level:** K–12 and adult
> **Coverage:**

- Historical information
- Images and explanations of U.S. paper currency
- Materials to order or download in multiple languages
- Lesson plans associated with National Standards
- Interactive notes featuring all denominations from $1 to $100
- Videos
- Games
- Virtual tour of coin production
- Information on counterfeiting and damaged currency

At the top of the BEP homepage under the *U.S. Currency* tab there are links to information about each denomination of the U.S. currency. Click on any denomination from one dollar to the one hundred dollar bill to find out the history of the currency and see a front and back image of current and past notes. Each description also includes the security features of the note in question. If you examine the PDF about the security features on the one-dollar bill, you will find that this bill has remained the same since 1963 because it is infrequently counterfeited. The security features include the serial number, the type of paper used, raised printing, and various seals. On all other currency except the two-dollar bill, there have been several security updates. The $500, $1,000, $5,000, and $10,000 notes were last printed in 1945 and were discontinued in 1969 due to lack of use. This is the kind of information you will find at the BEP site that will pique student interest in the national monetary system.

At the *U.S. Currency* page you can also choose *Training and Education* from the list at the left of the screen. This takes you to the BEP U.S. Currency Education Program *Resource Center* page that includes training materials for employees of cash-reliant industries such as banks. At the top of the page choose the link for *Materials to Download*. On the next screen, choose *Know Your Money* to see detailed illustrations of the different denominations of bills with highlighted information about each feature. These are available in a variety of languages. Be sure to specify your language of choice. Choose the specific denomination at the top of the U.S. Currency Education Program *Denomination* page to find printable descriptions of currency or access interactive note tutorials under *Security Features* at the *Resources* link. These allow students to explore the different security aspects of the currency such as watermarks, security ribbons, color shifting ink, and more. The interactive notes are available in several languages and all are provided as PDF downloads highlighting key security features for each note. There are also other brochures, posters and booklets available for download that may be useful in the classroom.

THE FEDERAL RESERVE

The Federal Reserve, or "the Fed" as most of us have heard it called, is run by a seven-member board of governors appointed by the President, each holding office for 14 years. The President nominates his choices and the Senate confirms each appointment. Members of the board represent a broad range of financial interests and geographic areas of the United States. No two members can be from the same Federal Reserve District. There are 12 districts spread across the nation and designated by number and by city. The Federal Reserve website hosts a number of award-winning educational tools (Board of Governors of the Federal Reserve, 2016).

URL: http://www.federalreserve.gov
Grade Level: K–12, college, and adult
Coverage:

- FED History
- Economic research
- Personal finances

The best way to find educational resources about the Fed is to go to its homepage and go to the site map link at the top left. Once you are on the site map page, scroll down to the topic *Publications and Education Resources* toward the bottom of the page. You'll see that *Education Resources* is your second choice of subtopic with several links listed. Start by picking the first link, *FED 101*. This takes you to a special website hosted by the Fed that is devoted to educational materials (https://www.federalreserveeducation .org). At the top right of the page you can search for resources *By Audience* (K–adult) or take a look at the *About the Fed* page.

Choose *By Audience* and select from the drop-down list to zero in on a specific grade range. The next page gives you a list of lesson plans, guides, and activities. At the left of the page you can narrow the search by grade, type, topics, and standards. If you click on *Lesson Plans* you can see the whole list of possibilities. There are K–4 resources based on picture books, some suitable for the 5–8 age group as well. For example, Judith Viorst's "Alexander Who Used to Be Rich Last Sunday" provides a lesson on counting and saving and planning for financial future. When Alexander receives a dollar from his grandparents, he tries to save it to buy a walkie-talkie, but he ends up spending it little by little. As children hear the story and do the activities associated with the lesson, they will learn how many pennies are in a dollar and what happens to the dollar when pennies are slowly subtracted from its value. There is a link for a PDF of the lesson and related activities, including the National Standards and Common Core Standards addressed in the lesson. The lesson is hosted at the Federal Reserve Bank of St. Louis website. Another lesson using the book, "Less than Zero," is a joint venture of the Federal Reserve banks of St. Louis and Philadelphia. A third lesson using the book, "On the Court with Michael Jordan" by Matt Christopher, targets 5–8 grades and addresses the National Standards for economics.

In total there are 194 lesson plans included in the K–12 list covering topics such as monetary policy, economics, financial fundamentals, banking, and information on the Federal Reserve. Perform a search using the limits at the left of the page. For instance, if you choose *Audience*: K–4, *Type*: lesson plan, the *Topic*: money, and *Standard*: National Jumpstart Standard: spending and saving, you'll find several lessons that meet those criteria, one of which is "Bunny Money." As in any advanced search, be careful not to overdo the limits on the search or you may find nothing. As you search, you may find that it will be possible to combine lessons to meet your needs. Try another search using only the categories *Audience*: K–4 and *Type*: *Activity*. This takes you to 52 resources including "Saving Strawberry Farm," a lesson that focuses on saving during the Depression. You can always go back to the main page and view the whole list for a specific audience to find elusive titles such as "Piggy Bank Primer," an ebook for children—available as a PDF file. Piggy Bank Primer can also be downloaded to iBooks on an iPad very successfully. Try a new search to see all available resources of a specific type by choosing *Video* and executing the search. You'll see a list of all videos provided, broken down by title of resource, audience, grade, and topic. At the top of this growing list of 110 videos you can find a video for the general public called "Buried by Debt." This video can be shown to high school or university students to spark a useful conversation about predatory lending, so much in the news in recent years. There are also informative videos on the creation of the Federal Reserve, the history of central banking, and early forms of money. Most videos are short and to the point, lasting five minutes or less. In a little over five minutes the video "Money: An Economist's Perspective" helps students learn about forms of money ranging from cows to cowry shells to the first coinage produced in the kingdom of Lydia, ruled by Croesus. This is a great jumpstart to understanding the expression "as rich as Croesus." The video also provides an opportunity to develop a conversation about forms of money in the United States throughout the centuries, such as wampum beads and tobacco. Students can think about and discuss what they currently value that might be considered a viable item for trade. It also could lead to a discussion of Bitcoin economy. Try searching by type for other resources ranging from lesson plans and activities to infographics and interactive games. Of course, the Fed also makes mobile apps available such as FRED (see Figure 7.1), an app that can be loaded to iPhone, iPad, or Android devices. FRED is a quick reference source for information on the following:

- Money, banking, and finance
- Population, employment, and labor
- National accounts
- Production and business activity
- Prices
- International data
- U.S. regional data
- Academic data

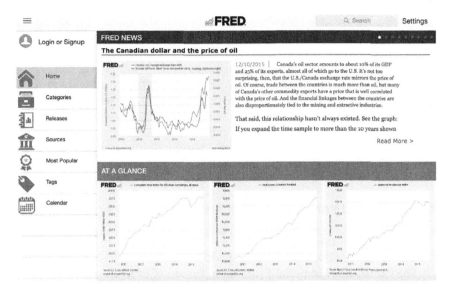

Figure 7.1 Featured App: FRED. ©Federal Reserve Bank of St. Louis. 2012. All rights reserved. Reprinted with permission of Federal Reserve Bank of St. Louis. http://research.stlouisfed.org/fred2/

MYMONEY.GOV

URL: mymoney.gov
Grade Level: K–12 and adult
MyMoney.gov is another valuable website for financial literacy training, produced by the federal Financial Literacy and Education Commission (FLEC). MyMoney.gov reflects the collaboration between 22 different federal agencies. The Secretary of the Treasury is the chair of the FLEC and the vice-chair is the director of the Consumer Financial Protection Bureau (CFPB) (Financial Literacy and Education Commission, 2016). The Mymoney.gov site highlights five financial principles: spending, earning, savings, and investment, protecting (identity) and borrowing. On the homepage, scroll to the bottom of your screen to see links to *Youth* and *Teachers and Educators*. The *Youth* link may be especially helpful for homeschooling parents who are looking for multimedia and other resources for their children.

There is a list of spotlighted resources divided by three categories: *Kids*, *Information for Parents and Kids*, and *High School Youth*. Each list provides a varying assortment of websites, games, videos, and articles. At the bottom of the screen is a "read more" link that accesses 50 other resources. These can be limited at the left of the screen by life event, *MyMoney Five* (referring to the five principles mentioned earlier), or topic, type, and audience. Each choice links out to information produced by other government entities. One example is *Youth.gov*, a site that is specifically directed to helping people create viable youth programs in their communities. Another linked site is *Benefits.gov* with information on government benefits eligibility. An important site for both parents and children can be accessed from the *Protect* category under *MyMoney Five*. "Help Your Children Grow Their Money Skills" is a product of the Consumer Financial Protection Bureau (CFPB).

CONSUMER FINANCIAL PROTECTION BUREAU

URL: consumerfinance.gov
Grade Level: Older students and adults
The **Consumer Financial Protection Bureau (CFPB)** characterizes itself on its *About Us* page as "a 21st century agency that helps consumer finance markets work by making rules more effective, by consistently and fairly enforcing those rules, and by empowering consumers to take more control over their economic lives." (Consumer Financial Protection Bureau, 2016) In this day and age we all need that kind of help, and the CFPB has been proactive in getting the word out to consumers that they can find support through their federal government. Versions of the website are available in eight languages other than English. Consumers are encouraged to lodge complaints and tell unique stories of their financial woes. This site is an education for any citizen. The *Educational Resources* link at the top of the CFPB homepage is a go-to place for everybody. Explore the drop down menu to find financial education resources for both adults and youth, resources for parents and resources for libraries. The *Youth Financial Education* link accesses resources specifically directed at students whether in college or getting ready to graduate high school and move on to college. The *Paying for College* link under the *Tools* section near the bottom of the page concentrates on understanding and navigating student loan debt as well as banking on campus. Some highlights of the student information to be gleaned from this site are a special section for student loan complaints, the college credit card agreement section, and the "Financial Aid Shopping Sheet," a PDF form found under *Know before You Owe*.

Paying for College

If a student is just getting started and doesn't know anything about paying for college, *Paying for College* is where to find answers to questions about types of loans, how to handle banking at the institution upon arrival at campus, and how to compare financial aid offers. Undecided students will benefit by using the *College Scorecard* near the bottom of the page to compare colleges based on the type of degree, location and size. Colorful graphs highlight the costs, graduation rate and potential salary after attending each college and students can look at the spread to make comparisons between schools. A *Details* link allows the user to see more information about graduation rates, student body characteristics, SAT and ACT score range and most popular academic programs. Encourage students to get to know the *Paying for College* page well. The time students put in to understanding the financial obligations before school starts will prevent many headaches further down the line.

Financial Aid Shopping Sheet

The Financial Aid Shopping Sheet can be downloaded from the CFPB site by choosing *Educational Resources, Youth Financial Education* and then scrolling down to the *Paying for College* link. Scroll down to the section called *Compare Financial Offers* and you'll see links to the *Know before You Owe* section and the *Financial Aid Shopping Sheet*. This form can be invaluable for individual students or families with a student headed for college. The form clearly sets out the various college expenses that a student can anticipate. The form was originally developed for colleges, and was intended to help them communicate their financial aid offers. Today it is being used in its final version by more than 1,800 colleges. For parents and students, seeing the form helps with understanding the complexities of what to look for in financial aid offers. The shopping sheet was developed with consumer input that can be seen at the CFPB site. There is a link to student loan information from the *Paying for College* page to see information about the FAFSA, student loans in the military, and student loan help available through public service organizations. Many public service agencies such as public schools, hospitals, and nonprofits offer student loan forgiveness programs for their employees.

Student Banking and Credit Cards

On the *Paying for College* page, choose *Student Financial Guides* and the link to *Student Banking*. This section is devoted to an examination of college agreements with credit card issuers, an explanation of how this can affect students, and a consumer advisory to students about their rights and options when it comes to student loan and scholarship access and use of credit cards on campus. Every page of the CFPB site has a *Submit*

a Complaint link at the top right. On the CFPB homepage choose *Data &
Research* to see another valuable resource, *Credit Card Surveys and Agreements*, a selection of databases with pertinent information on credit card
fees and interest rates and more. Here prospective students and their families can look for information on college credit card agreements. All of
these materials are worthy of close examination by students and their parents when applying to schools and considering offers.

Student Loans

The *Student Loans* page accessible from the *Paying for College* page under
Student Financial Guides also has valuable information for students about
comparing financial aid offers and repaying student debt. Follow the
tabs at the top of the page. Consumers can also examine a short analysis
of student loan complaint information after downloading the *Consumer
Response Annual Report* at the CFPB homepage under *Data & Research,
Research & Reports*. A careful study of all options on the CFPB site will
prepare both parents and students for all contingencies. Be sure to file
a complaint if necessary so that the CFPB can act on your behalf. The
CFPB provides a place for students to go to again and again to get the
answers they need and to lodge complaints when necessary. They will
likely want to come back to it later as consumers to glean more financial
advice from the site such as information on owning a home or to lodge
complaints about bad practices in the world of credit and debt.

DISPLAYS AND PROGRAMS FOR YOUR LIBRARY

Library patrons will thank you for any programs that you present to
help them understand how to improve their financial well-being. Most
parents take some trouble to introduce their children to the five concepts
on *MyMoney.gov*, and they welcome any reinforcement offered that will
interest their children. A display based on the five concepts of spending,
earning, saving/investment, protecting, and borrowing stimulates young
people's thinking in these areas. In such a display you could include some
of the picture books mentioned earlier in the chapter or other books having to do with money concepts. A piggy bank would add humor to the
display and could be the focus of a contest to guess how many pennies
are in the bank. The Federal Reserve Bank of Richmond provides a series
of downloadable bookmarks of famous Americans at https://www.rich
mondfed.org/publications/education/historical_figure_bookmarks/.
Download the Alexander Hamilton bookmark for a display featuring his
role in developing our financial system. His portrait is on the 10-dollar

bill, so you can add some currency to the display as well. Now that Hamilton is famous as the subject of a Broadway musical, a display in his honor is particularly apropos. An exhibit on counterfeiting would fascinate children at the middle school age level. Check the BEP page for information on counterfeit deterrence and supplement the display with other library materials. BEP also provides shredded money for a price, enough confetti to enliven any display!

Invite your patrons for a demonstration of the featured apps, *EyeNote* and *FRED*. EyeNote is an app from the Bureau of Engraving for the blind and legally blind. The purpose of the app is to help these users identify paper bills accurately. The user must allow the app to access the camera function and then hold the phone over the bill for the camera to read the image. A voice describes the bill denomination and indicates whether front or back of the bill is showing. It is simple to use but the user occasionally might have to back out of the app and reopen it to get an accurate reading of the next bill. This can be avoided by holding the phone at a far enough distance from the bill to make the whole bill visible on the screen. It also helps to have the bill lying flat on a surface.

Collaborate with a high school or university economics teacher to explore the attributes of FRED, and create a presentation for students or the public to go along with displays centered on the Federal Reserve. FRED shows quick snapshots of economic trends. Data can be accessed through a category search from the drop-down menu at the upper left of the app, and covers eight categories ranging from banking to production and market activity and prices. The user can search both U.S. regional data and international data. There is also a separate category for academic data. The user can search U.S. regional data by state, Census regions, Federal Reserve Districts, and so on. This can be an educational opportunity especially for high school age students who can use the *Most Popular* list of datasets found on the main drop-down to retrieve information for a targeted assignment. For instance, in the *Most Popular* list, the *Consumer Price Index for All Urban Consumers* shows a graph that can be manipulated to span from one year to ten years. Currently, the ten-year graph shows the large fluctuation that took place during the 2008 recession. In the *Notes* section, the CPI is explained in detail. The user can create an account and save data or share the data on Facebook and Twitter or in an email from which the user can download the graphs to a computer. FRED provides students and other patrons with an opportunity to see real data right on their smart devices.

The availability of online resources for financial information takes this search out of the realm of the esoteric and makes it doable for a determined student or consumer. The materials created for small children at the U.S. Mint and the Bureau of Engraving and Printing provide young people with a basic understanding of money and the economy to prepare them for more sophisticated resources later in life. The access provided for children at an early age can stimulate thinking and remove barriers to understanding when they are older and asking the harder questions. These agency websites are bound to change over time to include more resources. When children develop an early understanding of how to pursue a search on any government site, they are more likely to go back again to seek new information.

REFERENCES

Board of Governors of the Federal Reserve System. "About," accessed May 17, 2016, http://www.federalreserve.gov/aboutthefed/default.htm

Consumer Financial Protection Bureau. "About Us," accessed May 17, 2016, http://www.consumerfinance.gov/about-us/

Financial Literacy and Education Commission. "About Us," accessed May 17, 2016, http://www.mymoney.gov/Pages/About-Us.aspx

U.S. Department of the Treasury. "About," accessed May 17, 2016, https://www.treasury.gov/about/role-of-treasury/Pages/default.aspx

U.S. Mint. "About," accessed May 17, 2016, https://www.usmint.gov/about_the_mint/

8

More Government on the Web: Agency Pages, Digital Information, Apps, and Mobile Sites

The Government Publishing Office is mandated to move government information to the Web and has been doing that very effectively for the past few years. They have partnered with the Federal Depository Library Program to bring digital collections of government documents to the patron. As demonstrated in previous chapters, the various government agency pages have links to publications specific to their mission. Many more agencies provide small collections of educational materials to explain their mission or provide lesson plans for relevant content. Government agencies have also been building apps and mobile sites at a rapid rate. Many of the apps are specifically directed at children and young adults as well as at others and are usable at the university level. Apps and mobile sites provide great ways to serve the needs of students who are increasingly using mobile technology on a regular basis. Some of these have been highlighted in each chapter of this book. This chapter takes an in-depth look at more government agency pages, apps, mobile sites, and other digital materials.

Digital collections hosted by various FDLP libraries and government agencies are often motivated by government document librarians who are trying to make the best of the best accessible in a world that is increasingly dependent on technology. Librarians know well that the print medium has become inconsequential in many people's lives. While some librarians bemoan that trend, they also know that it is important to embrace the new technology and encourage information literacy for all citizens. Educators and students can benefit greatly from using a combination of agency websites with education links and information collected in digital collaborations between educational and government entities. Carefully selected apps and mobile sites can be intriguing not only to students but also to their parents.

Many of the new government digital resources that have become available to the public are the result of successful partnerships between government information librarians and the GPO to make materials available at the click of a mouse. Along the way advocates of the availability of more digital government resources have faced multiple problems, ranging from economic constraints to creating legible digital copies of archived materials; from questions of Internet security to concerns about preservation and conservation goals. Given the volume of government information that has traditionally been sent as paper copies to the over 1,200 FDLP libraries, this changeover to digital resources has taken place very quickly since it started in earnest in the early 1990s. Consider the partnership between the GPO, the United States Commission on Civil Rights, and the Thurgood Marshall Law Library at the University of Maryland for example (2015). They set out to provide access to important documents of the Commission on Civil Rights, starting in 2001. In 2007 the GPO put out the introductory press release to the public announcing the collaboration and the accessibility of these documents. In the intervening years many decisions had to be made.

Each step along the way to creating a digital collection is fraught with difficult choices. Expensive digital technology must be purchased. Experienced staff members who have been dealing with paper resources are called upon to learn the new technology and perfect skills to make digital copies that are easily accessible and legible online. Sometimes new hires are necessary or new positions created often stretching resources. In the early years the technology was cumbersome and always changing and it continues to change. Librarians have to face decisions about how to preserve the original documents such as whether to chop off spines of books to make it possible to copy the pages. Libraries committed to hard copy access must find ways to preserve paper copies, sometimes more than one. None of these are easy decisions and it all takes time.

The general public has no idea of the layered task presented when the decision to create a digital collection is made. The first task that faces the collaborating entities, beyond the obvious need to establish operational roles, is to corral the documents themselves. This may not be as easy as it sounds. Of course there will be some documents that are neatly cataloged and filed away, but there may be many others that are lost in someone's personal papers or tucked away at a government agency office. A librarian facing a digital project first has to look at what is in the main collection and then start filling perceived gaps. Some documents have become "fugitives." This is the term used by government information librarians for documents that have disappeared because they were never cataloged or made available through the FDLP. Some may have been privately funded, or are kept in the agency archives. When it comes time to digitize a collection, these documents must be found. Many of them have been unearthed over the years and have been cataloged by FDLP librarians.

When a collection is chosen for digitization, it is often a collection that has been carefully nurtured by librarians over the years. An example of this is the Southern Oregon Digital Archives (SODA) Bioregion Collection at Southern Oregon University (http://soda.sou.edu/). This is a collection of bioregional documents unique to the local area gathered over a span of 25 years. Every step of the creation of the SODA Bioregion Collection was hampered by the issues mentioned earlier (Hollens, 2006). Many FDLP librarians regularly track and capture fugitive government documents with digitization in mind. Even so, a collection may still have some outstanding publications that must be found before the digitization process can begin. If publications have been authored outside of the government agency, copyright permissions are needed. This is only the tip of the iceberg, presaging a whole series of decisions that have to be made and hurdles that must be surmounted to achieve the end product. Ideally that product is a seamless database with easy links to accurate digital information that reflects that best of the best of a legacy collection.

Why is this important for education? What use are these materials to our students? For a start, the information-seeking behavior of the average student, as described in the Introduction of this book, demands that these collections not only be available online but be pristine. Students will first go to Google, Yahoo!, Bing, whatever they favor. They will take whatever they find. If they are finding archival copies of primary source government documents, they will use them. However, if they find Joe Blow's website that haphazardly includes materials out of context from various sites, including government collections, they're just as likely to use that. As students are educated about how to find and use free government information, they learn the value of these primary and secondary source materials. They become discerning, information-literate individuals. Engagement with digital government collections teaches young people about the history and culture of the United States, and the principles of democracy through interaction with valid resources. Students then become thinking individuals who learn to scrutinize information, carefully evaluating what they find for authority, accuracy, currency, and objectivity. Eventually the practice of these skills will help them make informed decisions about their lives.

MORE GOVERNMENT AGENCY SITES

Central Intelligence Agency (CIA)

URL: https://www.cia.gov/index.html
Grade Level: K–12, undergraduate, and adult

Many students become fascinated by the CIA when they begin to understand its clandestine nature, and they might question its sketchy past. Go to the site map and find the *Kid's Zone* link for resources covering K–5 and 6–12 as well as teacher and parent guides. The K–5 page show pictures of the CIA Seal, gives information on dogs used by the CIA, the *CIA K9 Corps*, and includes a picture of each dog and a short autobiography. *Birds Eye View of CIA History* shows aerial photographs of CIA buildings, an interactive tour, and includes games with word finds, coloring activities, and so on. The 6–12 resources are more text-based resources about the CIA. Parent and teacher resources include specific 30- to 45-minute lesson plans.

For older students, including undergraduates, the most important CIA resource is the *World Factbook*, accessible on the homepage under *Resources*. The *World Factbook* provides information covering the history, economy, geography, and other basic facts about each of 267 countries.

Environmental Protection Agency (EPA)

URL: http://www3.epa.gov/
Grade Level: K–12, undergraduate, and adult
Go to the A–Z list for the EPA and look under E for education to find environmental education resources. On the EPA *Environmental Education* page you will find links to lesson plans, homework resources, videos, games, and more. Specific lesson plan packets, such as the one provided for acid rain, are quite thorough and provide experiments and activities as well as follow-up materials for further study. Resources for children range from coloring book activities to more sophisticated online sites such as *RadTown USA*, an interactive online book for kids to discover information on the presence of radon in our living and work environment. As of this writing, the EPA is improving the website and URLs are changing, so expect new resources in future.

Federal Bureau of Investigation (FBI)

URL: https://www.fbi.gov/
Grade Level: K–12 and adult
Go to the A–Z list or site map to access the *Kids Page* for the FBI. This page is divided into resources for K–5 and 6–12. The site is directed at students and their parents and includes games, safety tips, and information about FBI dogs for K–5, while the 6–12 resources concentrate on the history of the agency, description of investigative procedures, and the *Agent Challenge* page, where the student answers questions about the FBI and can check answers immediately.

U.S. Department of the Interior

URL: https://www.doi.gov/
Grade Level: K–12, undergraduate, and adult
Coverage:

- Environment
- Ecology
- Marine science
- Mapping resources
- Cultural resources
- National parks resources

The U.S. Department of the Interior was created in 1849 to address the internal affairs of the nation (Department of Interior, 2015). As it turned out, this became a complicated job. When you go to the Department of Interior homepage, go to the site map and notice the list of bureaus as you scroll down the page. Some are better resources than others for providing educational materials, but it is worth taking a look at all of them. A few of these are described next:

Bureau of Indian Education (BIE)

URL: http://www.bie.edu/
Grade Level: Not fully developed.
This site seems to be under construction. Although there are links for educators and educational resources designated by topic, there is little information provided. Check the Reports link and the Programs link to get an understanding of issues of Indian Education.

Bureau of Land Management (BLM) (Learning Landscapes)

URL: http://www.blm.gov/wo/st/en/res/Education_in_BLM/Learning_Landscapes.html
Grade Level: K–12 and adult
The BLM Learning Landscapes page has resources for teaching in the classroom and in field classrooms on the land. From the main page, there is a link to *Teachers* to find a variety of resources for environmental education. *Hands on the Land*, an independent program accessible from the BLM *Teachers* page, offers field learning experiences for children K–12 on 57 sites located in various areas of the United States. *Hands on the Land* is sponsored by Partners in Resource Education, a collaborative effort

between five federal agencies, schools, and other participants. The BLM site also offers *Teachers Guides* on various subjects, such as native plants and wilderness, as well as virtual field trip resources and a database of standards-based activities. Also, be sure to check your state BLM web page for local opportunities.

Bureau of Ocean Energy Management (BOEM)

URL: http://www.boem.gov/
Grade Level: 9–12 and adult
This site is appropriate for older students and educators or parents researching very specific information. The educational resources can be found through a site search on education. Also, look under the *News-room* tab to find *Factsheets, Statistics, Videos,* and the publication *Science Notes,* a brief quarterly publication that examines ongoing ocean research projects.

Bureau of Reclamation

URL: http://www.usbr.gov/
Grade Level: 9–12, college, and adult
There are no lesson plans or specific educational materials at this site. It would be helpful for high school and college age students interested in environmental policy and the conservation of water resources. Under the tab *Resources and Research,* look for *Environmental Resources/Reports* to find excellent information on environmental documents for your region. This is a good site for students who want to explore information on environmental policy and law in the National Environmental Policy Act (NEPA) Handbook.

National Park Service (NPS)

URL: http://www.nps.gov/index.htm
Grade Level: K–12 and adult
The National Park Service website provides tabs for both teachers and kids with information about the National Parks. In fall of 2015 they launched *Every Kid in a Park* in honor of the 100th anniversary of the National Parks. This is a new program designed to give every fourth grader an opportunity to act as an ambassador to bring their families to explore the National Parks for free between September 1, 2015, and August 30, 2016 (National Park Foundation, 2015).

U.S. Fish and Wildlife Service (USFWS)

URL: http://www.fws.gov/
Grade Level: K–12
When you go to this site, scroll down the list at the left side of the page to the category *Kids, Educators, Parents* to find an array of resources for outdoor learning and fun. There are games for the kids, curricula for teachers, and ideas for families about outdoor activities.

U.S. Geological Survey (USGS)

URL: http://www.usgs.gov/
Grade Level: K–12 and undergraduate
Standards: Next Generation Science Standards
Education resources are easily accessible from *Science* link at the top of the USGS homepage. Choose *Education* at the lower right of the drop-down menu. On the Education page choose resources by grade level: *K–6, 7–12,* and *Undergraduate.* You can check out the most popular resources from the photo links to videos, lectures, citizen science, maps, images, GIS resources, *USGS Kids,* and more. Break out your 3-D glasses to check out the interactive maps under *Park Geology in 3-D.* When you choose an age spread, the next page offers a list of resources in particular subject areas. You'll notice at the top of the page that symbols are designated to show if the lesson contains a complete teaching module, class activities, digital data, or images, or if it necessitates the purchase of optional items. When you look at the list and choose a subject such as "Become a Phenology Observer," the link takes you to a new page at the *National Phenology Network* that allows you to specify grade level, type of resource, or audience, or look for a particular resource by number. In this search you will find that some phenological lesson plans and activities do specify Next Generation Science Standards. The caveat is that some resource links go to error pages or may link to a new page with links that no longer function. This is the luck of the draw when it comes to electronic resources. Even so, following the links will help you discover other agencies and organizations of interest, as well as viable teaching materials. When links don't work, try finding the originating agency or organization through another search. While many of the searches in USGS lead to off-site Web material, others lead you back into USGS. An example of this is "Wise Wetland Ways," listed under the main heading *Ecosystems* on the K–6 page. Click on this link and you will access a USGS poster with activities. Another useful USGS page is "27 Ideas for Teaching with Topographic Maps." Of course map resources are the business of USGS, so you'll want to pay attention to all that are available.

U.S. Department of State

URL: http://www.state.gov/
Grade Level: Middle school and adult

Find the *Youth and Education* tab at the top of the U.S. State Department web page to access a variety of links. Click on more in the drop-down list to see all the resources. Students will benefit from looking at the *Discover Diplomacy* link. They can watch a one-minute video about the meaning and goals of diplomacy. *Diplomacy 101* is a lesson module that introduces students to the concepts of diplomatic action. Finally, they can navigate an interactive map of the world to find out about the people, places, and issues involved in diplomatic exchange.

For educators, the *History of Democracy* link accessible by choosing *More* in the *Youth and Education* drop-down goes to a page most valuable for its history curriculum guides. The *History of Diplomacy* curriculum packet was provided for a video once available from the State Department with an extensive script included and lessons to support the material. The curriculum guide is still available in PDF format. There are also links to curriculum guides for a variety of CD-ROM presentations that are no longer available, covering subjects as variable as sports and diplomacy, terrorism, and 200 years of relations with China. A quick look at the primary source list in the History of Diplomacy curriculum packet may jump-start your thinking for a lesson. The political cartoons that are included may encourage your students to think about current political cartooning and inspire a class to develop their own political cartoons. There are many other resources worthy of mention on this site, such as information for students on studying abroad and of course the *Country Profiles* section that help students learn about other nations. *Country Profiles* can be found by scrolling the right side of any page. Select a country from the drop-down to read about our relations with that country. The country profiles link out to more agency-generated information such as the CIA's *World Factbook*. Another area of the page worth exploring is the *Careers* tab for Foreign Service Officer career track, possibly of interest to students who are would-be international travelers. Have students explore the *13 Dimensions*, to test themselves on the qualities demanded of a foreign service officer. All of the qualities listed fulfill the needs of just about any occupation.

U.S. Institute of Peace

URL: http://www.usip.org/
Grade Level: High school and adult

The U.S. Institute of Peace links to education resources suitable for high school and above from the *Education and Training* tab at the top of the home page. Take a look at the *Teaching Resources and Simulations* to find a wide range of useful materials.

DIGITAL COLLECTIONS OF GOVERNMENT INFORMATION

Government documents are free and are part of the public domain and have been digitized by government agencies, educational institutions, and other organizations with mixed results.

Google Books

Google discovered the ease and value of digitizing government information early on. Since government information is in the public domain, what better way to populate a digitization project? A Google search often points users to Google Books, where they may find full or partial copies of digitized government documents.

HathiTrust

HathiTrust is a partnership of research libraries committed to digitizing items of cultural value (HathiTrust, 2015). In the case of HathiTrust, it was a natural choice to digitize government documents, once again because of lack of copyright restriction and wide availability of valuable government documents at FDLP collections in the participating research libraries.

Government Agency–Generated Digital Collections

Many government entities are digitizing their own collections. In some cases they do this because of their assigned role in gathering and preserving information. The Library of Congress, detailed in Chapter 5, acts as the national library and, in that capacity, preserves and makes available national historical and cultural information online in multiple formats. The **National Archives and Records Administration** is another agency with an active role in preserving historical documents. However, there are other agencies that also play a role in digitizing primary or secondary source documents that pertain to social, cultural, and historical concerns of the nation. As described earlier, the Office of Interior's National Park Service and the Environmental Protection Agency both publish digital materials on the environment. The U.S. Institute of Peace provides information on international conflict resolution. The U.S. Department of State also provides educational resources directed toward international policy.

It is not possible to detail each one, but if you go to the USA.gov A–Z list of government agencies you can find those that are not covered.

National Archives and Records Administration

URL: http://www.archives.gov/
Grade Level: High school, undergraduate, and adult
Standards: National History Standards

Another government entity that has developed educational materials related to its digital collections is the **National Archives and Records Administration (NARA)**. The NARA mandate is to preserve a small percentage of all government documents that are produced in this country based on the importance of the documents (National Archives, 2015). The title of the agency is descriptive but hardly romantic. It reflects the mission of saving in perpetuity paper documents that date back to the dawning of the United States of America. Now that the agency is digitizing some of these historic records, the American public has an unprecedented opportunity to view original materials from the comfort of home. This means that teachers can take advantage of these materials to enhance their classroom planning.

At the top of the NARA homepage is a direct link to teachers' resources. The main asset for teachers is *Docs Teach*, a site for history resources for the classroom. The *Docs Teach* page provides a *Find Activities* hot button to find tools for the classroom and a *Find Documents* button to find primary sources. The *Get Started* link at the left side of the page accesses an interactive learning module where teachers can customize lessons using the materials and documents provided. A teacher can register for *Docs Teach* for free and start creating activities or use activities that have already been created by other teachers using NARA materials. All of the lessons are linked to National History Standards.

For example, a lesson about the Great Depression and World War II includes the early and final drafts of President Franklin D. Roosevelt's speech announcing the attack on Pearl Harbor. Students are asked to look at these and decide on the three most important changes he made to the speech. Roosevelt originally wrote "a day which will live in world history." Now we remember the iconic text, "a day which will live in infamy." Students working within the NARA site and answering this question can email their answers directly to the teacher. In another activity students are given a document to examine together. They must decide about the significance of the document, a radar map of Oahu for December 7, 1941. In a third activity, students look at several documents and literally weigh the evidence on a virtual scale to determine whether Roosevelt's establishment of the Fair Employment Practices Committee

(FEPC) contributed to the subsequent Civil Rights Movement in the 1950s and 1960s. Another "weigh the evidence" activity pertaining to the New Deal includes primary resource documents, such as the text of a radio address given by President Roosevelt. He explains his decision to declare a bank holiday after the unprecedented run on the banks in March of 1933. Roosevelt's simple explanation of the principles of banking may be a revelation to many students. This is one of 15 documents and photographs that present the evidence students must examine, encouraging the concept of close reading and interpretation of the public record. There are many entries into the activities provided, including a browse feature that categorizes activities by *Historical Era, Historical Thinking Skill,* or *Tool.* The *Tool* list is divided into types of activity such as "Interpreting Data," "Finding a Sequence," and the aforementioned "Weighing the Evidence," among others. Users who register at the NARA education site have access to nearly 3,000 activities. Teachers are also invited to publish their original activities at the site. Registration allows users to save activities in an account or submit an activity for publication. The NARA site also has links to resources for National History Day, information on professional development workshops for educators, and educational resources from presidential libraries. Those who are located close to four NARA locations can take advantage of school visit programs in Washington, D.C.; Atlanta, Georgia; New York, New York; and Philadelphia, Pennsylvania. The other two locations—Kansas City, Missouri, and Seattle, Washington—provide telephone assistance with primary sources for college students and K–12 students researching History Day. The various presidential libraries listed on the NARA site also offer guided tours and programs.

The Digital Projects Registry

URL: http://registry.fdlp.gov
Grade Level: 9–12 and adult

The Digital Projects Registry is a listing of more than 150 publicly accessible collections of historical U.S. government documents that have been digitized in collaboration between government agencies, FDLP libraries, and other nonprofit institutions. The projects are divided roughly into seven categories; *Arts and Humanities; Business and Economy; General Interest; Legal and Regulatory; Natural Sciences and Mathematics; Social Sciences;* and *Technology and Applied Sciences.* The projects can be searched by category or browsed by project titles. Some collections appear under more than one category. The collection will continue to grow as more institutions commit time and resources toward this effort. Some examples are listed by category next.

Arts and Humanities

The Everglades Digital Library and America's Swamp: The Historical Everglades Project are both projects at the University of Florida. The Everglades Digital Library is a collection that documents the history and science of South Florida and provides datasets, maps, photos, and other educational materials concerning the area. America's Swamp: The Historical Everglades explores the impacts of early attempts at draining and despoiling the Everglades over the decades and the work of conservationists to save the swamp and its natural resources.

Klamath Waters Digital Library documents watershed issues in the Klamath Watershed of Oregon and is hosted by the Oregon Institute of Technology. The collection includes full text articles as well as photographs and maps from the 1800s forward.

The Ridgeway Brothers: Explorers, Scientists and Illustrators is a collection from Utah State University. As of this writing the link from the Digital Projects page leads to an error page. The collection hosts are responsible to send updated information to the GPO for the list and, perhaps, in this case the update has not been sent. Never fear, the title of the collection and the responsible party are listed for each project and it is just a matter of Internet sleuthing to find the Ridgeway Brothers at the Utah State University's digital project browse collections page (http://digital.lib.usu.edu/cdm/landingpage/collection/Ridgeway). It is well worth the trouble to discover the work of naturalist John and naturalist and illustrator Robert Ridgeway, two brothers who chronicled the American West in the late 19th century.

The University of North Texas, an early motivator of the move toward digital information, hosts several sites:

- FCC records
- Federal Newsmaps
- Soil Surveys
- World War Poster Collection.

The poster collection features over 600 posters from World Wars I and II. There are posters designed by famous artists such as Norman Rockwell and Theodore Geisel, better known as Doctor Seuss. Take a look at Dr. Seuss's "Starve the Squander Bug," encouraging people to buy war bonds during World War II. Students will enjoy seeing art work that was perhaps the precursor to the "Grinch Who Stole Christmas." The posters can be searched by country (some World War I posters were from France), decade, language, series title, or collection. Choose from various sizes to download an image.

Business and Economy

Here you will find digital collections from FRASER, an image archive from the Federal Reserve System that includes full text of Economic Indicators, Banking, and Monetary Statistics from 1914 to 1970 and All Bank Statistics. Also included are primary source documents related to the Federal Reserve Act, signed into law by President Woodrow Wilson in 1913. A fascinating study of women in labor is provided by the Publications of the Women's Bureau collection, also from FRASER.

General Interest

Depression and Panics is a general interest collection from FRASER that has valuable primary source information for high school and university students. The collection includes both government and nongovernment sources.

The Digital Library of the Caribbean and Panama and the Canal are both spearheaded by the University of Florida in collaboration with a number of institutions in the Caribbean and with the Panama Canal Museum.

Legal and Regulatory

Two collections that may be of special interest to high school students are "Early Recognized Treaties with American Indian Nations" from Oklahoma State University and the previously highlighted "Historical Publications of the United States Commission on Civil Rights" from the University of Maryland. Here also students can see the Public Papers of the Presidents, a vast stockpile of fascinating primary resources from the University of Michigan Libraries. It currently incorporates the privately published papers of FDR with the papers of all the presidents from Hoover to Clinton.

Natural Sciences and Mathematics

This is by far the largest of the categories and includes a number of watershed projects, digital publications from the National Forest Service, and USGS information, among other things.

One collection titled "Hurricane Reports" from the NOAA Central Library covers hurricane information starting with Edna and Hazel in 1954 and ending with Hurricane Katrina. The materials included are advisories and bulletins from the U.S. Weather Bureau. Browse the reports by date, hurricane name, or location.

Another interesting collection is the Digital Lunar Orbiter Photographic Atlas of the Moon from the Lunar and Planetary Institute. The collection is based on the Bowker and Hughes Lunar Orbiter Photographic Atlas and contains 670 stunning black and white images of the surface of the moon and explanatory text. This is a great site for moonstruck youth.

The Southern Oregon Digital Archives (SODA) from Southern Oregon University is made up of three collections that utilize government information extensively. The Bioregion collection highlights government publications related to the unique abundance and variety of plant and animal species in a small area of Southern Oregon and Northern California. The First Nations collection includes government documents pertinent to the local tribes. The History collection includes books, maps, government documents, and oral histories of early Southern Oregon settlers.

NOAA's "Why the Weather" is a collection of short essays by scientists Charles Franklin Brooks, founder and secretary of the American Meteorological Society, Alfred H. Thiessen, and Charles Fitzhugh Talman. These were composed between 1923 and 1941 as daily public service announcements to help the general public understand meteorological concepts. In his 1934 essay "Damp Weather and the Automobile," Talman explains why cars of the day run more smoothly but less efficiently in wet weather. In a 1935 essay, he explains the "Desert Mirage" phenomenon in two paragraphs.

Social Sciences

There are 29 sites included in this list, some repeats from other categories. Many of these are concerned with military history. One example is *Historic Government Publications from WWII*, hosted by Southern Methodist University. The site includes American propaganda from the war, pamphlets, speeches, and miscellaneous government reports. One pamphlet that might stimulate some thinking is titled "A Short Guide to Iraq," published in 1943 by the Special Forces Division, Army Service Forces, U.S. Army. The pamphlet admonishes soldiers to engage with the Iraqi people and to accept that there are differences in the way the Iraqis live and behave. The pamphlet goes on to describe the country and its importance to the war. It is laid out very simply at a high school level, aimed at the 18- and 19-year-olds who went to World War II in record numbers. Iraq was a strategic part of the war since Hitler was expected to try to come through Iraq to get to India. It also was a place through which the Americans could funnel supplies to their allies at the time, the Russians. The pamphlet also reports on the vast oil supplies of Iraq (United States, 1943). This pamphlet could spark fascinating discussion about our motives then and now in engaging with the Iraqi government.

Another site that will be useful for any lesson on World War II is the Topaz Japanese-American Relocation Center Digital Collection, hosted by Utah State University. This site includes Executive Orders 9066 and 9102, the order to establish the camps and the second order to establish the War Relocation Authority. Also included is the Civil Liberties Act of 1988 acknowledging the injustice of the relocation, making a formal apology, and establishing an education fund to inform the public so as to prevent a recurrence of something similar. This is an important act for students to see and understand in the context of anti-Muslim sentiment after 9/11.

Technology and Applied Sciences

There are 16 sites included in this category addressing a variety of scientific information spanning the subjects of aerospace and aviation, engineering, computer science, and artificial intelligence. A few sites stand out as especially useful for the classroom: the *Arpanet Archive* resources that document the beginnings of the Internet; *NASA Images; Organic Agriculture Information Access; and the USDA Pomological Watercolor Collection,* a fabulous collection of over 7,000 watercolor paintings of fruits and vegetables created between 1886 and 1942. Of these over 3,000 are images of apples! No wonder apple pie is an American staple. Gravenstein apples are favored for their tangy flavor (see Figure 8.1).

Figure 8.1 Gravenstein Apple, Artist: *Steadman, Royal Charles, b. 1875.* "U.S. Department of Agriculture Pomological Watercolor Collection. Rare and Special Collections, National Agricultural Library, Beltsville, MD 20705."

FROM APPLES TO APPS: GOVERNMENT RESOURCES ON SMART TECHNOLOGY

As is clear from previous chapters, cognizant of the trends toward the use of smart devices for everything from restaurant reservations to research at the restaurant table, the government is moving many resources to apps and mobile sites as quickly as it can. Many of these are tracked by the Federal Government Mobile Apps Directory (see Figure 8.2).

Federal Government Mobile Apps Directory

URL: https://www.usa.gov/mobile-apps
Grade Level: 6–12 and adult

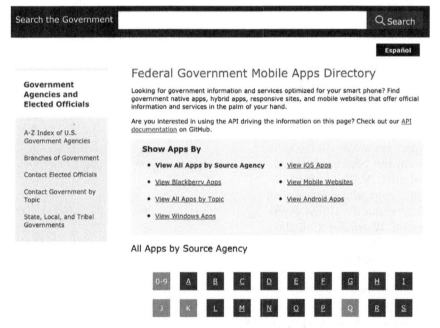

Figure 8.2   USA.gov Mobile Apps Directory: Did you know that if you made a free government app available to your patrons once a week, it would take the better part of three years to use up all the government apps and mobile sites?

Coverage:

- Art
- Aeronautics and space
- Criminology
- Defense
- Education
- Energy
- Government
- Health and food safety
- History
- Labor relations
- Science and environment
- Statistics
- Veterans affairs

The government started creating apps early in the days of the iPad and soon discovered the limitations of a static app. By 2012 agencies were emphasizing mobile sites. Since then government agencies have been creating apps and mobile sites for a variety of technology. The preponderance of available apps are for iOS devices, but there are also Android and Blackberry apps. At the *Mobile Apps Directory* you can access them by choosing a specific device, source agency, or topic. At the time of this writing, there are over 200 federal government apps for iOS devices, 127 for Android, and 6 for Blackberry. Ninety-one of these are mobile websites. This list will continue to grow and change. The Federal Registry for Educational Excellence (FREE), although still listed under Mobile Websites, is no longer viable, but points you to other possibilities. Some apps are not on the list at all, such as the Titanoboa Monster Snake Game from the Smithsonian. This was linked to a particular Smithsonian exhibition in 2012 and is still available on iTunes. Keep in mind that apps will probably come and go over time.

An example of this is the **MEanderthal** app. This is listed on the *Mobile Apps Directory* under Smithsonian but is no longer viable and has been taken off the Smithsonian page. It may be under reconstruction or may be replaced by another exhibit-related app. The *MEanderthal* app was linked to an exhibit, "What It Means to Be Human," at the Museum of Natural History. *MEanderthal* received quite a bit of attention when it first came out. Voted App of the week by YALSA on February 16, 2011, *MEanderthal* made it possible for young people to take a picture of a friend and then transform the image into the visage of an early human (YALSA, 2011). There is still information about the exhibit at the *Human Origins* website (http://humanorigins.si.edu), including lesson plans for teachers.

The National Museum of Natural History is a treasure trove of exhibit-related educational materials and provides an *Education* tab right at the top of the page. Apps and mobile sites from the government may come and go but they do still keep coming. If you are using mobile technology, watch Smithsonian and government agency pages of interest for new ones and don't expect them all to show up on the *Mobile Apps Directory*. Even so, the *Mobile Apps Directory* is a good place to start your research. There you can find the apps listed by agency and learn what government agencies interest you most. The apps range from single-topic informational products such as **PTSD Coach**, aimed at military veterans, their families, and others who need help coping with PTSD, to more layered applications such as the iPad app **Docs Teach** from the National Archives, a learning module that provides activities and primary source materials related to U.S. history.

More favorite apps and mobile sites are listed next:

- **Set in Style**: An app from the Cooper-Hewitt National Design Museum that gives a glimpse of the classic early 20th-century jewelry of Van Cleef and Arpels of Paris. The style of this jewelry profoundly influenced 20th-century decorative arts. It includes audio and video.
- **FBI Mobile**: This site covers the range of functions performed by the FBI and includes a *Quick Facts* page, an FAQ page, and information on the history of the FBI. It also has a *Sex Offender Registry* searchable by state. It is quite extensive and easily navigated by topics on the left of the page. It is especially good for students who are interested in criminal justice careers.
- **Congress.gov Mobile**: A go-to site for information about both current and past legislation, roll call votes, committee hearings videos, and nine videos that explain the legislative process by which a bill becomes a law, highlighting the unpredictability of that process.
- **American Red Cross**: The American Red Cross provides four apps, one giving updates on shelters called **ShelterView**, one called **First Aid**, and two more addressing safety information for hurricanes and tornados. Most are available on both Android and iOS technology. **ShelterView** is only available on iOS.
- **ATF—Bureau of Alcohol, Tobacco, Firearms and Explosives**: Available on Android and iOS technology, this app outlines the history of the ATF and also gives information on legislation affecting their mission. The main history page has simple links to various topics with short explanations. The topics covered are, Alcohol and Tobacco, Firearms, Lab Services, Arson, and Explosives. One

that might be interesting to students is the Badge History that includes information about the Internal Revenue Service authorization to investigate alcohol tax evaders that eventually led to Prohibition. There is also a firearm identification guide available. All links are accessed from the bottom of the screen.

- **Centers for Disease Control (CDC).** The Centers for Disease Control makes several apps available in the directory. These include the following:

  - **FluView** (iOS only): This app maps flu cases across the United States.
  - **Health IQ** (Android, iOS): This app provides an interactive game to test what you know about health. The game is set up at easy, moderate, and hard levels, and the user gets points for correctly answering question such as, "What is the minimum SPF needed to protect yourself from the sun's harmful rays?" Students can have fun and learn important information for a lifetime.
  - **CDC Mobile App** (Android, iOS): Access CDC information about disease and prevention quickly and easily through your smartphone or tablet. The information includes health articles as well as up-to-the-minute information about current outbreaks of disease. There is also a **CDC Mobile Web** site. **Solve the Outbreak** is an interactive app from the CDC aimed at students at the middle school level or above (see Figure 8.3).
  - **TravWell** (Android, iOS): A great app for international travelers. Plan your trip and get information on necessary vaccinations for your destinations. Store documents in the app at your discretion. There is a disclaimer when you first open the app that does not guarantee their safety. Students could use this app as part of a larger lesson on international commerce and travel.

- **Ask Karen—Department of Agriculture (USDA)** (Mobile Web, iOS, Android): Students can ask Karen question about how to cook foods safely and get tips on foodborne illness.
- **Breathe2Relax—Department of Defense (DOD)** (Android, iOS): Introduce this tool from the DOD in a health lesson to help your students learn how to relax through deep breathing. Experiment for a week with half the class using the tool and half going through the day in the usual way and discuss what happened after the trial. Did they notice a difference in their stress after learning a new way to breathe? How can they apply this information to their daily lives on a regular basis? How can they help their friends who are suffering from stress?

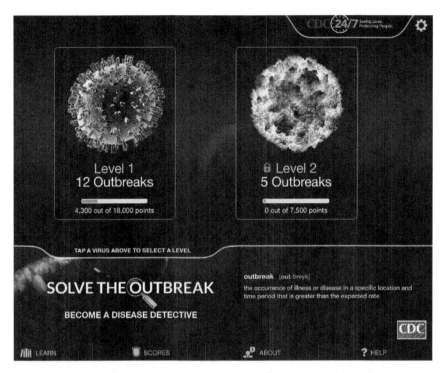

Figure 8.3   Highlighted App: Solve the Outbreak. This app motivates young people to learn how to analyze available data to investigate the cause of an outbreak and stop the spread of disease. *"Solve the Outbreak application developed by the Office of the Associate Director for Communication at the Centers for Disease Control and Prevention (CDC)."*

- **Brrrd Brawl—Department of Health and Human Services (HHS)**: This iOS app from HHS features turkeys and penguins battling it out with the help of some smothering hens who lay eggs at an alarming rate. Keeping up with eggs falling from above and the battle in view is no easy task. This is an app from teen.smokefree .gov and links to information about smoking cessation on the start page. The app is suitable distraction for people aged 10 to 90 if you don't mind participating in a battle of the birds.
- **Smart Traveler—Department of State** (Android, iOS): Keep up to date with country information, travel warnings, and information on embassy and consulate locations. After choosing a country, interested students can look at seven categories of information about the country, including a basic description, information on visa requirements, alerts about local laws, and health information. Use this as a teaching tool to open up students to a global perspective.

- **The White House—Executive Office of the President** (Mobile, Android, iOS): Have your students follow the White House blog for a few days and discuss what they are learning from the posts. It is particularly interesting to see how things change between one administration and the next. The Briefing Room is a good place for students to see primary source material as events occur such as remarks by the president and presidential proclamations. Students can also see pictures and videos from the White House on either the apps or the mobile site.
- **Smokey the Bear—U.S. Forest Service (USFS)** (Mobile, Android, iOS): The mobile app is limited to safety tips, a current wildfire map and wallpapers for kids that can be saved to your pictures. If you access the site on a desktop or laptop, you'll find that it is rich with content for both students and teachers, linking out to various resources such as a teaching guide on native plants from the BLM. Many of the resources can be accessed after clicking on Smokey Kids and then choosing from several categories offered. One of these is Forest Links, a section that provides links to Learning Landscapes for Kids with teacher guides, Kid's Wildland Fire Books with links to more information for teachers, and a collection of smokejumper photos among others items. As in some of the other older sites, the links are not always viable but there is still enough here to make it worth your while. Smokey's Journey, accessed as a tab from the main page, provides an interesting historical view of the development of Smokey Bear between the 1940s and the present. Old photos and radio interviews are included along with newer posters and videos. This might be an interesting lesson for high school students who have an interest in forest history, marketing, and wildfire prevention. Students could be tasked with analyzing the old advertising and comparing it with new wildfire prevention promotion techniques. Does Smokey the Bear still work as a concept?

The apps and mobile sites listed earlier are only a small sampling of what is available. As of this writing the *Mobile Apps Directory* does not seem to be stable: here today, gone tomorrow. If you see this at any government site, you can contact the site manager and ask questions. You will receive an answer that will help you understand the situation. In the case of the *Mobile Apps Directory*, for instance, the lack of stability is something they are aware of and are in the process of rectifying. You may be the first to alert the site manager to a problem, so it is always advisable to take the time to draw attention to problems. Look for a *Contact Us* or *Site Manager* link to follow through with questions.

Mobile Apps from Agency Sites

It is important to remember that if you are looking for apps on specific information, always check related agency websites to see what they have that is new. The best way to do this is to check the site map or A–Z Index for "Mobile." If you can't find anything there check the tabs at the top of the home page or scroll to the site links at the bottom of the page. If at a total loss, try a search in USA.gov for the name of the agency with the keyword "Mobile." Every agency is slightly different. For instance, at the CDC site you will find the apps through the A–Z Index at the top of the page but at the USDA website, you're better off using the site search box. The Smithsonian has a "Connect" link at the bottom of their home page that leads to a page with links to social media and also mobile applications. The Smithsonian even has an "Apps for Apes" program using apps with Orangutans. The primates enjoy playing with iPads held for them by their trainers. They enjoy music apps, drawing apps, or even just watching fish swim. The Smithsonian is accepting old iPads for use with the apes if you are looking for a worthy cause and a recycling opportunity. As mobile technology becomes more sophisticated, and users find new ways to employ it, government agencies will continue to make these available.

All the resources mentioned in this chapter will change over time but the method of finding them probably won't alter considerably. The most important thing to remember is to look for government information where it is most likely to be found, at an agency or agencies dedicated to the issues or topics concerned. If you don't know the agency, check the agency list at USA.gov to get ideas. Mining government agencies for information can be a very rewarding activity. When you are at a loss, it may be time to take advantage of the services offered by your closest federal depository library and talk to an FDLP librarian.

REFERENCES

Covintree, Kate. 2011. "App of the Week: MEanderthal," *Young Adult Library Services Association YALSBlog*, accessed May 17, 2016.

HathiTrust. "Welcome to the Shared Digital Future," accessed January 7, 2016, https://www.hathitrust.org/about

Hollens, Deborah. 2006. "The Southern Oregon Digital Archives: Unique Opportunity and Continuing Challenge." *OLA Quarterly*, 12, no. 1: 16–18.

National Archives and Records Administration. "About the National Archives," accessed January 7, 2016, http://www.archives.gov/about/

National Park Foundation. "Every Kid in a Park," accessed December 23, 2015, http://www.nationalparks.org/ook/every-kid-in-a-park

Thurgood Marshall Law Library. "Historical Publications of the United States Commission on Civil Rights," accessed December 29, 2015, http://www.law.umaryland.edu/marshall/usccr/

United States. 1943. *A Short Guide to Iraq.* Washington, DC: War and Navy Departments. http://digitallibrary.smu.edu/cul/gir/ww2/pdf/w0025.pdf

U.S. Department of Interior. "Who We Are: History of Interior," accessed December 29, 2015, https://www.doi.gov/whoweare/history/

9

Finding the Needle in the Haystack

When you can't find what you are looking for or can't interpret what you find, it is time to consult a federal depository librarian. FDLP librarians are trained to understand what is and what is not available and where. Electronic information is layered and often users are able to access only the very superficial layer at the top. This is especially true of government documents. Government documents have morphed from messy piles of paper in FDLP library documents departments. Now they are found both in paper and as a scattering of online links that often seem to have no rhyme or reason. This is slowly sorting itself out over time, but with the plethora of information generated by a myriad of government agencies, much information is buried. FDLP librarians also spend an inordinate amount of time chasing what they call "fugitive" documents. These are documents that have been produced by government agencies but have never been cataloged through the GPO. Due to the heroic efforts of FDLP librarians, these fugitives, including important scientific reports, are captured and cataloged for all of us to find. Users may come across a mention of such a document and be unable to find it until an FDLP librarian enters the fray.

RELY ON THE EXPERTISE OF AN FDLP LIBRARIAN

Depending on the size of his collection, an FDLP librarian can either find a paper document for you in house or request help from other FDLP librarians throughout the country. This is a loosely knit group of dedicated people who have learned to take great joy in tracking the vicissitudes of government. They make it their business to understand their own collections while maintaining close contact with each other to keep the information lines open. The FDLP librarian has a mandate to serve her constituency, and is therefore accessible to all citizens of the local congressional district. She may not have the answer for you right away, but can usually meet your needs after some strategic sleuthing.

As is true of information gathering in general, search strategy is important. Even the best of online searches often leads to dead ends. Government information slowly and belatedly entered the online world starting in the mid-1990s. This slow pace of online adoption reflects a large and unwieldy data set that continues to change at a fast rate. The result is that government information resources online are relatively young and mutable. In the 20 years of the transition to an online platform, government entities have had to absorb major technology changes and catch up to the users. Add to that the fact that budgets have been shrinking during the most recent of those years and it is no wonder that you find quite a few dead links at government agency sites as personnel scramble to move to new platforms. The GPO changed its name from Government Printing Office to Government Publishing Office only at the beginning of 2015, an official, if belated, nod to the move from printing to digitizing government documents.

During the transition there has been a major shift in the world of FDLP Libraries. Many more libraries are choosing to go with all electronic collections even while maintaining a basic historical print collection. This makes it possible for more libraries to be involved at a smaller level with targeted electronic collections. On the downside, librarians who have been the guardians of historic paper collections face a dilemma. These collections contain everything from the 1950s and 1960s congressional hearings pertaining to the Mafia to a 1920s agricultural pamphlet on how to raise pigs or a 1930s Depression-Era booklet on the WPA. Some of these older documents are gems in our collections and not all have been digitized. The only way to find this older historical information is to consult with an FDLP librarian.

GOVERNMENT DOCUMENTS IN POPULAR CULTURE

As a member of the Permanent Subcommittee on Investigations, Chief Counsel Robert F. Kennedy led congressional hearings pertaining to Mafia kingpins in 1959. Later, in his capacity as Attorney General of the United States, he used the evidence gathered to prosecute members of the mob. The investigation ultimately led to the Racketeer Influenced and Corrupt Organization (RICO) provision in the 1970 Crime Control Act (144 Cong. Rec. 1998). Who could predict that these same documents and original television footage of the hearings would be featured as a prominent tourist exhibit at the Las Vegas Mob Museum in the 21st century?

There are many examples of ways that an FDLP librarian can help with a variety of personal research projects. A historian looking for old railroad surveys from the 1800s was thrilled to find one available as part of the *U.S. Serial Set* in a depository collection at a New Mexico university. The item in question was a beautiful book painstakingly illustrated with botanical drawings made by the U.S. survey team as they discovered a pristine new wilderness. Although it was on the shelf, this document was not cataloged. This is not an unusual occurrence with older documents. In such a case it takes the expertise of a documents librarian who knows the collection to find what is needed. Scientists looking for obscure agency reports often resort to the federal depository librarian to find materials since the items are not always cataloged by title but must be tracked down through knowledge of the series that contains them. An entrepreneur looking for statistics for a demographic profile of the local area sought help from an FDLP librarian in Oregon when contemplating a new start-up business. A former student at a small university came to the FDLP librarian looking for the yearbook of his graduating class of 20 years previous and was thrilled to find it in the FDLP librarian's state documents collection; so thrilled, in fact, that he donated money to the university library. Now that same individual can see the yearbook in a digitized collection online. The list of ordinary citizens who stop by an FDLP library for help is never ending.

Top Ten Reasons to Consult with an FDLP Librarian

1. You're completely new to government searching and don't want to waste time.

Perhaps a patron has come to you asking for some specific government information. If you feel flummoxed by the question, don't hesitate to call your closest FDLP librarian for help. If the library is close enough, send your patron on to the librarian.

2. You want historical congressional information that you cannot find online.

Historical congressional information is not necessarily readily available online. For instance, the *Congressional Record* provides important primary source materials, tracking the daily decision-making process and the roll-call votes in Congress. The GPO's Federal Digital System (FDsys) has digitized daily *Congressional Record* information for 1994 to the present and an index spanning 1983 to the present. For any years pervious you will need the bound copies to be found in most FDLP libraries that still maintain historical print collections. Eventually more of these will be digitized. Until then the FDLP librarian is your best bet.

   3. *You are trying to find specific statistics for your town and have not had success.*

Patrons believe that the *Census* is the be-all and end-all for statistics at all levels. In fact, *Census* statistics, although surprisingly robust, do have their limitations. Bear in mind that these statistics are taken on the national level and may not reflect the kinds of information that may be better sought in state and county statistical databases. FDLP librarians are savvy when it comes to identifying at which level of government an issue becomes important. They also can help the user interpret the statistical information provided or identify a state, county, or city agency that may have more information.

   4. *You are looking for government statistics but have had no luck tracking them down.*

Patrons often do not understand that the government is a statistical gold mine. They also don't know how to go about searching for statistics. Often patrons will read a secondary source in paper or online that quotes government statistics but gives sketchy attribution. Many librarians can spot this easily. However, an FDLP librarian will immediately be able to track down the pertinent government agency and unravel the problem. An FDLP librarian also can recognize when a statistic would more likely be collected at a state or local level.

   5. *You want to identify a government agency that might have the information you need.*

The list of government agencies is long and can be somewhat impenetrable for someone who is trying a quick search. An FDLP librarian will be able to identify not only the agency but also the pertinent level of government, saving much time and agony for the patron.

   6. *You would like to understand the processes behind congressional actions and the making of laws and feel a bit fuzzy.*

FDLP librarians have a good understanding of the legislative process and can easily access information from FDsys, Congress.gov, and other sites to help a patron understand the workings of government. They also have access to handouts and materials that illustrate the information.

7. *You are studying history, political science, military science, or any aspect of law and need primary sources.*

Government documents supply primary source material for in-depth study of the legislative process. FDLP librarians are adept at helping users with finding information on legislative history. They also host important resources in their collections. such as the *Statistical Abstract of the United States*, older editions of the *Statutes at Large, and* military history resources from the *Department of Defense.*

8. *You are trying to find a particular document that you find mention of online but no digitized copy.*

Patrons may be trying to track a reference from an article available online or may have found a partial copy of something related to government information and would like to see the whole document. FDLP librarians can quickly track the information down in their own or others' print or digital collections.

9. *You prefer a paper document to the online source.*

There are patrons who prefer to read paper, rather than online, sources. This is especially true of government documents. Many government documents are hundreds of pages long and difficult to page through on a computer. An FDLP librarian may be able to provide the paper document alongside the online version and show the patron how to search in the online document for keywords, to effectively use these resources side by side.

10. *You are looking for state documents information that you cannot find online.*

Many FDLP libraries also house state documents collections. State documents collections are increasingly going to an online format but the historical documents are not necessarily digitized. Also, an FDLP librarian can quickly identify if information should best be sought in the federal or state collection and save patrons valuable time.

Join the FDLP!

Find out if you are close to an FDLP library by checking the Map of FDLP libraries on the GPO's Federal Depository Library page (http://www.fdlp.gov/about-the-fdlp/federal-depository-libraries). If you are managing a public library that is far from an FDLP library or you find that the FDLP librarian is sometimes too busy to give you a timely response, consider joining the FDLP yourself to take advantage of available federal government resources. This also provides you with the opportunity to reach out more widely to the incredible network of FDLP librarians all over the country. This may seem far-fetched to you. Perhaps you think you are too small to consider such a radical step. Do you have 10,000 books in your library and a patron base that is looking for health information or statistical information? Do you have businesses that need your information-gathering expertise to consider regulatory and legal ramifications in their day-to-day work? If so, you may be the perfect candidate to host a small, electronic-only FDLP library. It takes no physical space and it expands your outreach to patrons. The next chapter explores this possibility and gives more details on how you can join a dedicated group of librarians working to make a difference in information dissemination for our democracy.

REFERENCE

144 Cong. Rec. S182-S183 (January 28, 1998) (remarks of Senator Susan M. Collins), accessed January 22, 2016, https://www.gpo.gov/fdsys/pkg/CREC-1998-01-28/pdf/CREC-1998-01-28-pt1-PgS182-2.pdf

10

Joining the FDLP: Are You Eligible? What's in It for You?

To maintain its status as the largest publisher in the world, the GPO must effectively distribute this excess of free information to the public through a system that also supports each patron's understanding of how to use it. This is where the Federal Depository Library Program (FDLP) comes into play. Currently there is an unprecedented opportunity for smaller public libraries to be players in the FDLP community. For one thing, they are now able to choose to receive only electronic documents, posing no space impact for libraries that are emphasizing user comfort and maker spaces in their buildings.

CONSIDER YOUR OPTIONS

The first thing you need to know if you have interest in becoming part of this robust distributorship is that the GPO hosts an FDLP page that tells you all about it. The FDLP page is where to start and where you'll come back to again and again to understand your role and responsibilities once you have signed on as an FDLP Library.

GPO's FDLP Page

URL: http://www.fdlp.gov/
Coverage:
- FDLP Basics: Learn about the program.
- FDLP Quick Start Guide: How to proceed after becoming an FDLP Library.
- Join the FDLP: Basic information and guidance on how to join and benefit from partnering in the FDLP.

- Collection Tools: Drop-down list of essential tools for documents librarians
- Requirements at a Glance: Drop-down list for all aspects of FDLP requirements
- About the FDLP: Drop-down list for basic information, events, training, and more
- Cataloging and Classification: Important information on cataloging for your library

The FDLP provides you with an opportunity to enhance your catalog with electronically accessible information from government agencies, congressional primary source materials, and much more. At your discretion, you can also choose to stock some print materials on your shelves. These can be purchased from the GPO Bookstore or gleaned for free from Offers lists regularly put out by larger FDLP libraries. Of course there are some parameters to which you must adhere. This list of basic requirements to get started, as shown next, is available at the FDLP page.

Understanding the Basic FDLP Requirements

URL: http://www.fdlp.gov/join-the-fdlp

- Maintain a collection of at least 10,000 books (i.e., print and microfiche information products), other than the federal government information products received through the FDLP.
- Provide free **public** access to the federal documents collection and public access workstations.
- Process, catalog, and maintain federal materials in a timely manner and within prescribed guidelines.
- Understand and comply with the legal regulations of the program.
- Have knowledgeable reference staff that are trained in the use of depository information resources.

As you can see from reading the list, you will likely have some questions as to what it all means. For instance, you may ask yourself, "Who are my public?" "How do I set up a public access work station for government information?" and "How can I train my staff?" All of the answers to your questions can be clarified with careful study of the FDLP site and thoughtful questions to GPO personnel. The GPO is eager to advise you. Your staff will benefit from a new-found ability to help patrons with a whole different level of expertise that can positively impact their daily lives, whether they are dealing with health problems, immigration issues, or garden pests.

Who Is Your Public?

As a public library, your patrons come from the city and county in which your library resides and, for the most part, these are the people you will be serving also as an FDLP Library. However, you will also serve the larger congressional district. You may get more or fewer questions depending on the proximity of a more robust FDLP collection. Bear in mind that when you feel out of your depth, you can refer users to the more extensive FDLP library. Whatever the case, you will have at your disposal the larger world of the FDLP to help you tackle the harder questions and to meet the needs of your patrons.

Collection Development

When considering collection development issues for your library, you will benefit from demographic studies of your patron population just as you would for your general collection. Think of your local, county, and state geographic and demographic makeup to guide you through these choices.

- *What type of industry and business are you supporting with information resources?*

For instance, if mining is an industry in your area, you may want historical reports from the U.S. Bureau of Mines available from the Department of Commerce National Technical Information Service (NTIS). You'll also want to access the U.S. Geological Survey National Minerals Information Center for data.

- *Are you in a coastal area or mountain locations with specific environmental concerns that may be answered by government information resources?*

In those cases, Environmental Protection Agency or Department of Interior documents may serve your users.

- *Do you have a high population of one or another ethnic group?*

You may then want to take advantage of resources supplied in alternate languages by various federal government agencies.

These are questions that only you can answer, and the answers will point you to the right choices for your patrons.

Cataloging Your FDLP Collection

Cataloging for your new electronic collection of FDLP documents can be solved by checking your eligibility to join the FDLP Cataloging Record Distribution Project (CRDP) to receive free cataloging through a partnership of the GPO and MARCIVE Inc. Depending on the size of your FDLP profile and the set of materials you choose to host, you can decide on other cataloging options for your library.

Training

The new *FDLP Academy* (http://www.fdlp.gov/about-the-fdlp/fdlp-academy) is an excellent source for training materials for you and your staff. The GPO has partnered with FDLP librarians to deliver targeted presentations on a variety of topics. The *Academy* provides regular webinar sessions that are accessible to you and anyone in the general public. Archived webinars are accessible to anyone so you can start looking at these to inform your decision process.

Start your training with the excellent webinar presentation from November 3, 2015, "Government Documents for the Masses: Collection Development for the Public Library." This presentation not only gives guidance on collection development decisions, but also gives you the perspective of a longtime FDLP public librarian, Karen Heil (Middletown Thrall Library, Middletown, NY), and her unique relationship to her user base. It is a joy to see how she was able to create a specialized government documents collection that attracted her users with "fun" items as well as nuts-and-bolts documents.

The second presenter, Tom Fischlschweiger (Broward County Main Library), gives detailed instructions on how to navigate some of the tools provided on the FDLP page. You'll see how one 50-minute webinar can put you on the right track with a wealth of information to get you started in your role as FDLP librarian. Initially the extra investment of time may seem daunting, but it pays off when patrons are able to get the help they need at the tap of your fingertips (FDLP Academy, 2015).

Plan Ahead

Keep all the aforementioned information in mind when making your decision and, meanwhile, get to know the FDLP community. If you have the opportunity and are willing to spend some time and resources, attend an annual conference in Arlington, Virginia, and plan to visit the GPO in Washington, D.C., while there. The more you know before you dive in, the better off you will be. Government information librarians are a passionate group who are more than willing to share their knowledge and expertise. If you are unable to travel far, seek out another FDLP library close to home. Be prepared with questions that you have about the program. To read the latest about government information check out the ALA Government Documents Roundtable (GODORT) wiki (http://www.ala.org/godort/dttp/aboutdttp) and read the newest as well as archived versions of "Documents to the People DttP," a publication featuring articles about federal, state, and international government information as well as issues faced by the FDLP community. After joining the FDLP you will be able to participate in list-serves that will keep you informed about what is going on in the world of government documents. Two of these are the GPO FDLP list (fdlp-l@gpo.gov) and a list for the discussion of government documents issues (GOVDOC-L@lists.psu.edu). There is much to learn from monitoring these lists, especially the second one where government documents librarians pose questions to the group about tricky reference transactions and more. Here, you'll also find information about hard copy documents that are on offer to other libraries, a source for free materials for your library.

Promoting Access to FDLP Collections

If you are interested in the advocacy side of government information provision, be sure to bookmark the *Free Government Information (FGI)* website (http://freegovinfo.info/) to keep up with various issues. This site is staffed by several dedicated volunteer librarians with the mission to provide a forum for dialog about provision of and access to government information (FGI, 2016). It addresses ongoing concerns that, with the transition to digital formats, citizens will lose free access to government documents if the GPO fails to establish clear preservation and access guidelines for both historical and born digital collections. FGI was given the GODORT "Documents to the People DttP" award for 2015. Read the main page to catch up on the latest discussions affecting the FDLP community. For fun, go to the "Best Titles Ever!" tab. This connects you to a Tumblr site that pictures a 1963 publication from the USDA, "Packet for the Bride," emphasizing what every new housewife will need to know! Even these minor publications are a goldmine of American cultural information. Efforts of FGI contributors and other librarians of the FDLP who have negotiated painstakingly with GPO over the years as members of the Federal Depository Council are essential. All of us have a stake in making government documents, available, understandable, and accessible to our users.

REFERENCES

FDLP Academy. "Government Documents for the Masses: Collection Development for the Public Library," webinar by Karen Heil and Tom Fischlschweiger, November 3, 2015.

FGI. "About," accessed May 17, 2016, http://freegovinfo.info/node/10

SELECTED RECOMMENDED READING

Ennis, Lisa A. 2007. *Government Documents Librarianship: A Guide for the Neo-Depository Era.* Medford, NJ: Information Today.

Forte, Eric J., Cassandra J. Hartnett, and Andrea Sevetson. 2011. *Fundamentals of Government Information: Mining, Finding, Evaluating, and Using Government Resources.* New York: Neal-Schuman Publishers.

Robinson, Judith Schiek. 1998. *Tapping the Government Grapevine: The User Friendly Guide to U.S. Government Information Sources.* 3rd ed. Phoenix, AZ: Oryx Press.

Conclusion

The tools in this book may help you to inspire young people to look to government documents for information at all levels of their education. As you pass on the information to students, educators, and parents, stress that government information is all-encompassing, data-rich, and free! The more your patrons appreciate and use government resources, the more chance there is of preserving the role of the GPO and FDLP as providers of essential materials that directly relate to our national history, identity, and culture.

Access to government information is an ongoing issue as budgets are depleted and much of the information is born digital. Considering technology, security, and digital preservation issues, the question is, Will these digital documents adequately replace their paper counterparts of old? Next time you log on will you be able to find your favorite site? Most of us already know the answer to that question having faced the frustration of searching the Internet. Old guard government documents librarians are worried that access to our historical print collection also may be compromised with a recent change in document discard practices. There is also concern about the disbanding of the regional depositories that traditionally housed one hundred percent of documents, accessible to the public. So although funding is at the top of the list, all of us should be fully aware of the other issues involved.

The government information community is grappling with the same problems that face the publishing community. After all, GPO is a publisher and, to meet the demands of the age, they have adopted a digital future for government documents. Smaller public libraries can become part of that digital future by choosing to join the FDLP. If you choose an electronic profile for your library, you've impacted no space and you can significantly add to your collection in a variety of subject areas. If you choose to select some paper materials, you may be preserving copies of important documents that would otherwise be discarded. Either way, your patrons benefit from the additions to your catalog and the new expertise of your staff.

The next generation of voters in the United States will thank you for helping them understand the workings of their government. They will also grow up with a deeper appreciation of the resources provided by all levels of government. Equipped with an understanding of agency hierarchies they will be able to navigate a plethora of scientific, statistical, and technological data. They'll have enjoyed the beauty and diversity of government program materials related to the arts and humanities. They may eventually become engaged in local, regional, and national civic improvement as a result of the understanding that government plays a vital role in their lives and their educational progress. The variety of materials on offer will appeal to all ages. Although this book has emphasized federal online resources, much of the online federal historical information is a facsimile of the real thing that may be found in a museum or library somewhere. The nature of human curiosity is to want to see the original. When we promote these online resources to children, we can spark that curiosity and grow informed citizens who will advocate for thoughtful promotion and preservation of government resources essential to the nation.

Index

About the Author

Dorothy Ormes, MLS, M.A.Ed., is associate professor and government information/instruction librarian at Southern Oregon University, Ashland, Oregon. She has authored several articles on teaching using government information resources. Ormes has presented at the Federal Depository Library Conference on three different occasions and was invited to present at the Arkansas Library Association Conference in 2013. She is past chair of the Documents Interest Group of Oregon (DIGOR) and has participated on the ALA Government Documents Round Table (GODORT) Education Committee. She is also an accomplished storyteller who has told stories in schools, libraries, and other venues for 25 years. In 2009, as Federal Depository coordinator at New Mexico State University, Dorothy produced a storytelling event for an ALA/NEH-sponsored "Soul of the People" Great Depression Road Show presentation, "Slaves, Sidekicks and Healers: Women's Stories Collected by the WPA" in Las Cruces, New Mexico, highlighting oral histories from the Library of Congress American Memory Project.